When Bonnie Cullen arrives in 1
of post-Franco Spain, a place where farmers scythe by hand, leap over
fires at Midsummer. Over the next four decades she will witness its
transformation into the clubbing capital of the world.

Cullen is a city dropout in search of a "more authentic" life. But how
to deal with an amorous shepherd, throw an American party for a
Spanish village, face the slaughter of your favourite pig? Years later,
she will have to confront a heroine from the Civil War and learn to
sleep when the thunk-thunking stops in the last club at dawn. Rootless
despite a deep attachment to Ibiza and its people, the writer revisits
two ghosts - an orchard and an ancient spring. *When the Water Speaks* is
a story of both person and place, dealing with change.

Bonnie Cullen teaches History of Art at Cuesta College in San Luis
Obispo, California. After graduating from the University of Chicago,
and working at the Victoria & Albert Museum and the National
Portrait Gallery in London, she travelled to Ibiza in 1976, where she
would live for nearly three years, teaching at Morna Valley School. In
1985, she returned with her family to settle in a small village until the
end of 1987. She has been visiting the island frequently ever since.

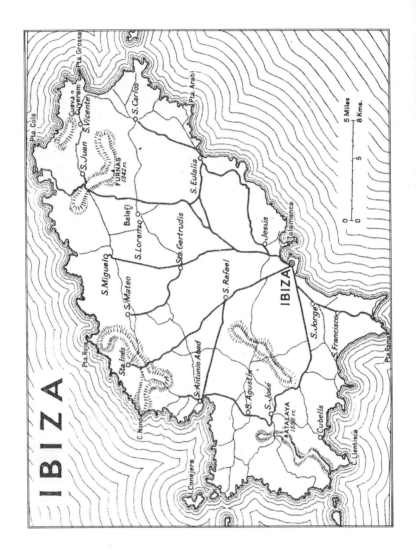

When the Water Speaks

A Memoir of Ibiza

Bonnie Cullen

Brimstone Press

Contents

Part I Long Ago

Part II Then

Part III These Days

For Vedra and Brigid

Part I: Long Ago

I

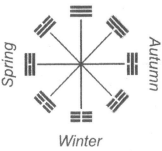

Summer

Spring

Autumn

Winter

The Beginning

TIME, THE SORT watches measure, had stopped. That was the first thing you noticed. Ibiza's pendulum was the sun and the seasons, and as you fell in with their slow-motion rhythms, your senses grew shoots and tendrils. Silence was a presence so thick and soothing that sounds rising- cicadas, wind, rain on baked earth - had an hypnotic effect. Rich and strange, too, was the lie of the land. Clusters of white cubes, each slightly different, rose here and there within a maze of fields, footpaths and wildflowers. Where one farm ended and another began wasn't clear. Stone walls corralled almond and olive, moulded terraces across slopes to the top, where only a couple trees could fit, and rambling over the land, they seemed to weave things together as much as separate them.

It was 1977, the first warm day in March as I remember, and we were tramping across a ridge on the north end of the island looking for the sea. Behind us was the stone hulk my friend and I shared with several people, and a day's worth of mop-and-bucketing. But here we were. A scent like sweet peas had blown in that morning and spirited us away.

In the valley below, a man and his horse were plowing red-brown snakes in the land. No machines, not a paved road as far as the eye could range. My American eyes kept on searching, for fences, *Private* signs. Not one. Some unknown force had beamed us up to Arcadia, apparently. I didn't know about my English friend, who had been there for some time, but I was a bit nervous about my good luck.

The year before, I had reached a dead end. It had started off well: a grant to study in Britain had taken me from Chicago to London. A couple of excellent jobs in art museums followed, but as my career blossomed during those years, a relationship became a dark prison with only one exit: leaving England, starting over.

For a while I worked on a scheme involving a small boat and the French canals. It got bogged down and there was a danger of not going at all. With a few pound notes and one memento, a Japanese parasol, I took a train heading south, hoping to survive for…well, I didn't know. Somewhere I would have to build a new life.

Near the Spanish border, the compartment filled up with a family who began passing round bits of sausage. The mother sliced off some bread and handed me pieces like a distant cousin. They did all the talking. I spoke little Spanish, but we grew friendly, breaking bread, and when everyone bundled out at a station some time later, the father pointed to a water tap on the platform, inviting me to join them.

There was a long line and a lot of bustle at the tap. I was just finishing my turn when the train whistle blew, and spinning around, I saw it head out, carrying the family and my bag with it. I charged down the platform, arms flailing.

The man in the uniform gave a polite nod to the only words that popped out the mouth of the wretch in front of his desk, *"Mon argent…le passeport…sur le train…"* He reached for the phone. How idiotic. Defining myself as a "traveler" (ah, hubris!) because I once hitch-hiked through Turkey and Bulgaria. And so on. Still, would a family man like that trick a young woman and steal her passport?

At last another train arrived and we reached the next stop. There was the bag, everything in place except for the parasol. Fair enough. If someone was willing to hand back my passport and money, they deserved a present. It was a good omen, I decided.

After that, things began to slow down, settle. Barcelona was wrapped in a daze and faintly exotic, its dark, empty passages smelling of urine. The hotel window opened to an air well of dripping underwear and on the bedside table where an ashtray might have stood, a clean sardine tin was offering its services.

While Europe had been forging an economic union, Spain was still cut off in 1976, languishing at the fag end of the Franco years. The Caudillo was dead, and to kick-start a new government, the king had appointed a premier, Adolfo Suárez. Yet development and democracy were still a mirage. A hundred kilometers offshore on the island of Ibiza, the long siesta of the mainland slipped into a dream: there were the inhabitants - scything, threshing with horses, butchering their own pigs, as they had done since the Middle Ages.

Shortly after landing, I met a Dutch family who offered a bed, outside beneath a shady fig. They survived by selling children's clothes at a market stall on the coast so I joined in, cutting tiny waistcoats and trousers and helping to look after their children.

By September, the tourist trade was fading along with what little money I had left. Not knowing what to do, I was following a philosophy we called "Be Here Now", good for staying calm and avoiding decisions. Sometimes. People in the market were closing shop, flapping their wings, talking of Nepal or Morocco. Like Marco Polo, they would seek out treasures and return to make their fortune next summer. My idea of business was to make and sell enough children's clothes for us to eat the following week. One evening at a party near the village of San Carlos, I met a woman headed for India. She was about to leave her job at a school for English-speaking children. It was not far away, she said. Why not talk to the headmistress?

"Mary's school", as people called it, was bursting out of an old farmhouse for lunch when someone strode into her office and began to explain why teaching a course on medieval manuscripts was good preparation for running a kindergarten. The woman behind the desk studied the applicant through enormous doe eyes, smiling. She looked remarkably serene for a headmistress. Without asking for documents, or even letters of recommendation, she took the risk. The position was part-time: kindergarten in the mornings, playground during lunch. Salary? About enough for food and a room.

I had just moved in with some Canadian and English friends who were renting a farmhouse about an hour's walk from the school. Relative poverty can be a good thing. Tramping the route, you watched figs and mulberries turn gold and fall asleep, and with the autumn rains, winter wheat sprouting in the fields. On fallow ground, lines of white sea squills rose like sentinels from enormous bulbs.

The artists shaping this terrain - rather squat, on average, and sturdy-looking under their straw hats - were remarkably good-natured about aliens popping up in the middle of it. Short of stomping on crops, you could put out a finger and follow it in any direction, pausing to talk with the *eivissencs,* as they called themselves, along the way.

Or rather, babble. The Spanish I was trying to learn kept bumping into another idiom. Because the island once belonged to a kingdom ruled by Catalans, Ibizans spoke a dialect of that language. Franco had imposed *castellano,* Spanish, on Catalonia by force and some of the old people hardly spoke it at all, so that, garbling new words, I met confusion everywhere. More often than not, everyone had a good laugh, and they would invite me in for a drink.

Something in their earthy-smelling houses triggered a memory: dozing in my father's cigar smoke… crinkle-faced farmers, joking in a language I didn't understand. But the eivissencs were a lot more jovial than our people, poor Swedes who left to try their luck in Michigan and Illinois. Nor were they as puritanical. Although officially they were Catholic, the farmers of Ibiza were far from narrow-minded. If they found me outrageous, a footloose unmarried woman, etc., they kept it to themselves.

In December came the winds, penetrating our stone house with a merciless damp. We'd moved again to an enormous and very old farmhouse. It straddled a ridge like a ruined fortress, tiny windows peeping out from a face of peeling whitewash. One barn-like room, housed the grinding stone where farmers from surrounding *fincas,* estates, once pressed their olives. The stone lay idle now beside the horse cart and sacks of carob beans our landlord fed his pigs.

Next door was the kitchen. You could have fed a village inside it, if you didn't mind the equipment, a row of fire pits along one wall. Overhead, a massive chimney flue spread out at the sides into drying racks where, long ago, farm boys slept among the hay. Or so I imagined. It was much too smoky when I tried it.

We huddled under that chimney on winter nights - six adults and two small children playing music, scuttling about the flagstones with pots of food, burning what wood could be scavenged (sweet-scented juniper on a lucky night). Like many other foreigners, we were often out of money. We had rejected "safe" career paths, and had plenty of troubles - friends in prison, fatherless children. Yet life was good. All around, nature ran its perfect cycles, nourishing our spirits. Tilling, planting, scything, the eivissencs seemed to accept our presence on their land, and our different ways. Perhaps they wondered why we all lived in the same house or who was married to whom, but they didn't ask.

One thing we and our neighbors had in common: food. Although they toiled well past sunset and were cash-poor, the people of Ibiza were finally recovering from years of famine after the Civil War. Of course our foreign money was easing their situation, but that only partly explains the way they treated us. Even before the war, outsiders of a different cast like Walter Benjamin, the philosopher and writer, encountered a laissez-faire style there. Benjamin, who was both Jewish and a communist, was running out of work when he left Germany for Ibiza in 1932. One of his best stories describes a customs agent in Ibiza helping foreigners dismantle furniture so they only had to pay duty on the boards.

That winter when the school holidays came, I spent a week in Barcelona. A friend knew a journalist from Argentina with an empty couch. I was hoping to learn a bit about Spain, as opposed to Ibiza. Strolling out onto the Passeig de Gràcia one evening, I saw a squad of police, riot masks on, truncheons raised, heading my way. Someone pulled me into a doorway just as they ran by, pursuing some invisible mob. On the Plaça Cataluna there was a large crowd on the side adjoining the Ramblas, more agitated than angry, it seemed, tossing a few beer cans into the air. People were still circulating on the Ramblas, the usual lovers and pedlars, but less of them, and more police. Then from one of the side streets, another squad of grey shirts, truncheons and guns. People ducked into cafés as the phalanx rushed toward its target, which was not, apparently, the crowd that had gathered.

Inside a café near the top of the Ramblas, people crushed the bar, joking, trying to look nonchalant. In fact, the air was electric with both fear and enthusiasm. It was anyone's call. Who could predict how much things would change after forty years of Franco? Spain had had more experience with *coups d'état* - in the last two centuries, at least fifty - than democracy. Already that winter there were rumors. Then in April, a bold move: Suárez (originally a Franco man) legalized the Communist Party. June brought the first democratic elections, with Suárez leading a new parliament. Four years later, however, gun-toting Guardia Civil would march in and hold the assembly hostage until King Juan Carlos opted for democracy, dismissing the officers who had orchestrated the coup.

All this lay in the future. Returning from Barcelona, I found Ibiza even more out of touch and Arcadian, existing in some other dimension, safe and sound. In February, pink and white almond blossoms draped the valleys. Then for the next two months, the earth put forth her designs, kaleidoscopic, evolving, as if, weaving a carpet on the fields, she could not decide the pattern: yellow daisies and mustard; wild garlic, mallow, and rockrose; blue borage and chicory, miniature irises; slender gladioli with magenta blossoms; white Queen Anne's lace and star-shaped asphodel. Finally, the climax: great splashes of poppy blood.

Of course we had squabbles, and every morning there were the lamp glasses full of greasy soot. It clung to the sides of the wash bowls when you scoured them with newspaper. Then we would load the laundry baskets and, children in tow, head out down the path toward the well. No matter the season, the water was always freezing. *Plonk* went the bucket, *swoosh*, up it came, *creeeeeek, creeeeeeking* through your arms as you tugged on the rope. We spent the rest of the morning in torrents of water, scrubbing clothes, dousing the children and ourselves.. On cold days it was torture, but more often than not the sun shone, and we stood protected by a ring of massive olives drying in the sun. We didn't talk about it, but I think focusing on fire and water, shelter and food, we were searching for a more authentic existence.

Still, unlike our neighbors, we were not tied to the land. Some of us rented a plot down in the valley and grew vegetables, but our survival did not depend upon it. Nor could we have lived like the farmers of Ibiza. Suspended between the modern world that had shaped us and the traditional rhythms of the eivissencs - up at dawn, shoulder to the plow - we feared, I think, that despite our illusions, many of us would be just passing through. That awareness was always in the background, a leitmotiv faint and bittersweet.

2

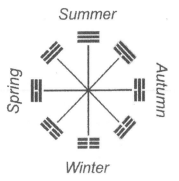

The Source

IN THOSE DAYS at the house we lived on beans and rice, or rice and beans. Not far away as we rustled up our daily grub, an orchard spilled its fruits downhill with the seasons. First, oranges and lemons. Then the loquats, apricots, cherries and pears, and finally, toward autumn, a gush of persimmons. Mature, noble, the trees stood in terraces cut into the slope, drinking from an ancient spring as it ran down stone channels. This fecund place, the *huerto,* belonged to our neighbor Jaime.

Now fruit was my weakness, had always been. As a child, I used to hide in the boughs of a cherry beside our house, devouring handfuls, envisioning paradise rather like Jaime's *huerto*: a forest dripping fruit onto the ground.

I began to prowl it at night. Now and then a shadow trailed me, jet black with a head like Anubis, that jackal god you see in Egyptian tombs opening the mouths of the dead. She was wild, a half breed marked by Ibiza's hunting hounds, the *podencos*. (Some traced the breed to ancient Egypt where the pygmy god Bes, who had a following on Ibiza, originated. In which case, both god and dog must have sailed in with the Cathaginians when they set up a colony here in the 7th c. BC). Gypsy - what other name for such a spirit? - was the wrong color and only half their size, but as springy on the chase, flying over brush like they did. A *podenco* sprite, you might say.

Our paths crossed one day in the woods where she was hunting wild rabbits. At that time I was traversing the valley on foot, walking to work or the town of San Carlos, or out to the coast. A network of trails wove hills and valleys together throughout the island. Entering the network was like being caught up in a current. You sped downhill, flowed through figs and oranges, rounded a corner, cruised past the front patio of a house and made for agaves lining a dirt road. It was strange at first, passing so near a house, but these were old ways, open to all. Crossing freely, merging with the landscape brought on a terrific sense of wellbeing, obliterating for a time the problems you had to face when motion stopped.

Sometimes I carried on for several days, staying with friends along the way. Gypsy's territory was the pine forests lining the hilltops. Whenever we met, she would follow me for a while until I shooed her away. Sometimes she slinked past our house looking for me, but she knew what farmers did to stray dogs. On our *huerto* patrols she kept watch, twitchy, knowing we were up to something, while I dined on the run, as she did in the woods. Our little secret.

Of course, Jaime would have offered a bagful from the orchard if anyone had asked for an orange. He lived in a *finca* uphill from ours. Occasionally we walked up there to buy eggs or their cash crop, almonds. This sent chickens squawking into the cactus, and hearing the commotion, his wife, Eulalia, would emerge from the metal fly curtains, smile, and cross her courtyard of potted plants to invite us in. They treated us as honored guests. We must sit down for a bit, sample the wine Jaime made, have some bread... On the way out, tomatoes or peppers were heaped on top the basket of whatever we bought.

Taken freely under cover of night, however, a neighbor's bounty is forbidden fruit. I couldn't resist it. The Puck in me, I suppose.

One morning, scouting the *huerto* on my way down the hill, I spotted Jaime gathering cherries in a basket. He must have been about sixty then. As a rule, eivissencs tended toward the short and stocky, but Jaime, lanky and spectacled with a frumpled jacket over his bones, looked more librarian than *campesino*. Not very nimble on the ladder, either.

Word had it that during the Civil War he was a key Republican. I wondered sometimes whether Jaime had hidden amigos in one of his sheds or in a cave I discovered nearby. The area where we lived around the town of San Carlos was known as a stronghold of old Republicans. Every morning in the town's only bar, the indomitable Anita would be sweeping last night's party out the door with the cigarette butts, hair falling with the effort. She was still waiting for her lover, a resistance leader in the Civil War, people said. The story was that just before the fascists arrived he had escaped, stealing a fishing boat and sailing single-handed to Algeria.

San Carlos was popular with fugitives as well. Many had fled dictatorships in Chile, Argentina, Brazil. Near the anarchical crowd who frequented Anita's, Spain's paramilitary police, the Guardia Civil, hovered like matadors in capes and *tricornio* hats. They flashed rifles and bullied anyone who fell in their clutches, but the eivissencs were an independent lot, opposed to control by outsiders, including the national police. You felt relatively safe there.

Nevertheless, you didn't ask people like Jaime about la Guerra Civil. In those days, the subject was taboo. If you did happen to mention it during a conversation with eivissencs, they inevitably muttered the favorite anecdote - how they survived by eating carob beans. And that was that.

Jaime had spotted me as well that morning, and waved me over. We exchanged the usual *buenas tardes* and remarks on the *buen tiempo*. For a farmer, of course, "good weather" meant nature doing as it should at that time of the year, whatever that might be. I was about to carry on down the hill when he looked over his spectacles directly into my eyes in a way he had never done before. "Would you like me," he said (arms sweeping tree-ward, mouth curling into a mischievous grin), "to lift you up, *señorita*, so you can pick some yourself"?

It was quite a performance, totally out of character. Jaime was a fundamentally decent man and no lecher, surely. Everyone had heard about the one eivissenc in the valley with a roguish reputation, a man called Pepe. Skewered with embarrassment, I realized that rather than flirting, Jaime was making fun of me, telling me, in a wily, old-fashioned way, "I know your nightly escapades, *señorita*, and I'm no fool."

So much for poaching. Yet the *huerto* carried on weaving its spell, and even after we all left the house that summer, I kept passing by day, following the water as it flowed down the long stone troughs to the terraces. At the top, feeding everything, was an ancient *fuente,* a spring, housed in a whitewashed chamber. It glittered within its tiny temple, the *genius loci*, spirit of the place.

However hot the sun, inside the chamber it was moist and cool.

A tunnel with stone steps led down to the *fuente*. The arc of the roof followed the slope, creating a low channel that ended abruptly at the water, as if directing those who entered to kneel when they reached the spring. It lay in a round pool, fecund and mysterious, fed by slits in the rock on either side and I remember two tiny ferns at the edge, waving in the current.

Around it, the walls glowed with reflected light. When you stepped into the chamber, they would respond, pressing echoes into your eardrums. At the bottom, kneeling, I would scoop water in my hands to drench my face. The sound as it fell seemed to strike my inner being, set me resonating toward the source. Strange as it may seem, I had the sense it was speaking, if only I could understand.

3

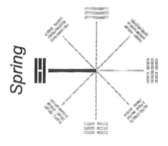

Spring

S'Hort

HAD YOU AND I been in Buenos Aires in 1908, turning, with our coffees, to a travel feature in the morning news, we would have read the following:

> The pistol is something like a second language to the Ibizan. In their traditional dances on Sunday afternoon, he moves with the agility of a clown while the beloved, eyes downcast, arms at her side, makes huge figure eights, her white shoes just visible under the balloon of the petticoats..... passion mounts with the encounters and frictions of this form, which is like a persecution through dance, and in the middle of the choreography, almost without interrupting it, he pulls out a pistol and dispatches two shots at the feet of the betrothed, who continues her steps, blushing and trembling with this amorous gesture. [Macabich, *Historia de Ibiza*, vol IV, p.17]

Even now, those Ibizan machos keep persecuting their doll-like partners. As far as anyone can tell, their traditional dance is unique to Ibiza and the neighboring island of Formentera. Perhaps it survives because it conveys an image of themselves they treasure: self-sufficient pirates, a bit rough about the edges. They've been perfecting this persona for some time.

In the Middle Ages when Spain was mostly Muslim territory, the Balearic Islands made an ideal base for grabbing Christian ships. Piracy was not just a Moor's game, of course. Not long after regaining the archipelago, the King of Majorca received a letter from Ibiza. The situation was desperate, wrote his newly appointed governor: Ibiza needed farm laborers tout de suite. Send off a pirate to the Barbary coast, wrote Jaime I, and fetch some more.

Strictly speaking, a "pirate" works for personal profit and outside the law whereas a "privateer" is authorized by some government. In wartime it depends whose side you're on. Take Barbarossa, the 16th century "Barbary pirate". His name sounds familiar, but how many people know Hayreddin Barbarossa began his career as a trader, took to privateering when his brother was snagged in a raid by the Knights of Malta, and ended up Fleet Admiral of the Ottoman navy?

When he got to Menorca and razed the main city, the Spanish ruler at the time, Charles the V, had had enough. Up went the battlements, including the massive walls encircling the old city, Dalt Vila, on Ibiza.

If you were left on the land, you made for the nearest town, and into the fortress churches in San Miguel, Santa Eulalia, or San Jorge. So it went, for generations. As the Spanish Empire disintegrated, Ibizans were left to defend themselves. They lit signal fires atop those towers standing tall along the coast. In the deep country, some of the houses had refuge towers built alongside. In went the families, climbing to an upper floor and pulling up the ladder.

Bravado grows fashionable after a while. Ibizans turned corsair and made their own daring raids. In 1806, a boat full of eivissencs took on a British ship while the crowd on the shore cheered. Into the twentieth century, the island's young men were still packing knives or pistols. A writer living there at the outbreak of the Civil War, Elliott Paul, would portray the fishermen of Santa Eulalia as lovable anarchists who smuggled tobacco on the side.

Toughness, the underdog taking charge, making his own rules - this became the Ibiza mystique. A place where the customs agent helps the little guy; a place, they still say, where orders arrive from "headquarters", but it is the locals who enforce them. Small wonder, then, that Ibiza appealed to a Marxist like Benjamin. Later there would be fugitives political and otherwise, and some tricksters. Clifford Irving, for example, who faked an autobiography of Howard Hughes and sold it to McGraw-Hill.

Another "Ibiza", one especially dear to Benjamin, is the island of self-sufficient farmers perpetuating ancient rhythms. "The island is really far removed from international trade and even civilization," he wrote to his friend Gerhard Scholem. "Three chairs along the wall of the room...greet the stranger with assurance and weightiness, as if three works by Cranach or

Gauguin were leaning against the wall". While peasants in southern Italy had to survive on one eighth of their output, sharecroppers in Ibiza were getting a house rent-free and half their output. Small farms gave, still give, the island a democratic feeling.

With the depredations of the Civil War, the scene Benjamin described changed very little for a couple decades. Then, among the crowds stepping off the ferries in the '60s and '70s came a new wave of leftists, larger and more diverse than the last. Exiles fleeing prison and torture in South America. North Americans and Europeans, seeking an antidote to capitalist culture, its spiritual poverty and "military industrial complex" feeding on war. If Marx and Trotsky were the focus in the '30s, now it was Che Guevara, Régis Debray and Malcolm X. But also Camus, Alan Watts, Ram Dass, Siddhartha, and Lao-Tzu.

Politics and economics, morality, social structures, religion: all were up for scrutiny. Both the "bucolic island" and the "anarchical pirate island" appealed to those who came looking for a place to reinvent the world. And so, nearly two years after my arrival, in a house somewhere between the towns of San Juan and San Miguel, we were listening with interest to an American named Ted...

"Simple - that's the beauty of it." Ted was grinning, as he often did, like a boy who's just been to the World Series and caught a home run into the grandstands. "Everyone puts in two hundred dollars. With this we fix up the place and set up the businesses. We've got an Austrian pastry chef, a Dutch restaurateur, and a Swiss herbalist. There's Sadid - fantastic leatherwork - and Alberto and Marielena. They'll run a boutique. And..." (the grin ate up the remaining space between glasses and beard) "we've got Black Bob. Can't miss. There's a shed a couple terraces down from the main building. Great place for a pottery, Jim."

Ted had recently joined a cooperative business that was starting up in the village of San Miguel. It was called "S'Hort", or "the garden", in eivissenc. Jim was a talented ceramist and he and I were together, looking for a house to rent. Meanwhile Ted and his wife Daphne were loaning us their trailer. Daphne taught

Spanish at Mary's School. Ted was pushing fifty, a "retired businessman" (he never got more specific than that) from California. After leaving suburban Los Angeles, they had "tried Amsterdam" where Daphne worked for a publisher, and were now trying Ibiza. Unlike most of the foreigners we knew, they owned their own house.

I was pregnant and still teaching, growing bilious in the hot rooms stuffed with children. Jim, the father of the baby, was the son of a British diplomat and not much given to manual labor, though he abhorred the privileged classes who had tried to mold him in a "sadistic" public school. As an artist Jim was gifted, but with the British economy in the deep-freeze, he was barely making a living. Soon we would have to survive on an editing job for a Dutch publisher that Daphne was sharing with me, and a bit of money he had brought from England. We didn't have two hundred to spare. "No problem," said Ted, and he handed over a fistful of notes.

S'Hort had just leased a bakery in San Miguel on the north coast. The village consisted of three bars, a grocery, a doctor's surgery, and perhaps a hundred eivissencs, all clinging to a slope below the fortress of their medieval church. The *panaderia* had been closed since the baker died. It was a giant version of those hive-like brick ovens one saw in the country, the sort grandmothers stuffed with wood to cook the family loaves.

The property included a substantial and very old house attached to the bakery. The facade was unimpressive. You might have easily overlooked it walking up the street. Inside, it was classic eivissenc: huge trunks of juniper suspended over stone walls. The walls were a meter thick or more, pierced with cube-like windows that let in shafts of light. This would form the hub, a vegetarian restaurant and bakery, with other businesses slotted into sheds and corrals on the terraces below. One area with a shady fig and a bougainvillea-covered wall could be transformed, via plants and built-in benches, into a tea garden.

Just whose brainchild S'Hort was, Ted didn't know, if I remember correctly. At point S'Hort was in the planning phase, with a projected opening around the full moon in June. Meetings, or what would later be called "brainstorming" sessions, took place every few days at a member's house or beneath the fig tree on the terrace. Judging by the way they perambulated the floor addressing the group, the major players appeared to be a madrileño named Sadid and a Dutchman, Jos. Sadid carried himself like a grandee, despite the bandana worn pirate-fashion over a beautifully chiseled nose. His English was mellifluous, ornate, like the designs he tooled on leather saddlebags. Jos, our future chef, was more intense, peering through dense lenses, eyeballs like bull's-eye marbles as he described the dishes he would concoct.

Butter-like, always smiling, Alberto and Marielena remained in the background tending to their several children. They had been in the clothing business for some time. Occasionally one would toss out a solution to something Jos and Sadid had been dissecting at length. That triggered head-nodding all round and I took it they were key members as well.

If he was feeling passionate, a German craftsman named Johan interjected a sentence or two. Franz, our Austrian baker, said very little. He was younger, early twenties, perhaps, and more articulate at cafes where we debated how to make the perfect pastry. Notably absent (he would be at some remote location delivering another baby) was "Black Bob". Bob had learned his trade "in a chopper over Vietnam", he said. He was the oldest, except for Ted, and because he had been in the trenches, respected by all. Charming, and relaxed, he looked to be the perfect Tea Master.

The women of S'Hort stood in the outer circle, observing what the italianas called the "cock parade on the floor." When the talk ended, the real work would begin and we would be doing plenty of it, was the joke. The only woman who sparred verbally with Jos and Sadid was a feisty Swiss named Heida. She and Corinne, Bob's delivery nurse, would be opening a medicinal herb shop.

S'Hort had a doctor as well, Roberta from Naples. She had just finished a degree in pediatrics and was applying for a license to practice in Ibiza. Since that could take years, Roberta joined S'Hort, she said, "so the boyfriend would have something to do". He, Nanni, was a kind of Italian Johnny Appleseed, planting rows of fava beans wherever he happened to be staying. A Marxist as well. Nanni didn't care who reaped the harvest. "If everyone tilled as they went, we would never be hungry," he was always saying.

Daphne did not have enough time, or perhaps interest, to be involved, but Ted had plenty of both, although he didn't appear at all the meetings. He wasn't sure what role he would play. "Consultant, maybe? Maybe just investor…" Not everyone would be running a business, as Ted explained it, nor would all parts of S'Hort be in operation at first. Members would be helping each other.

We must have discussed logistics from time to time but I don't remember anyone asking who held the money or how we would decide which businesses to develop first. There was no particular structure, no chain of command as far as I could tell. I wasn't even sure how many members there were. Decisions were achieved in an atmosphere of mutual accord, but not everything was discussed. We were questers, en route to a better world, itching to experiment, I think, and if we agreed on anything it was that greed and self-interest were driving the world toward destruction, and communal efforts were the way forward. Many were also travelers, used to situations demanding trust. Details would fall into place.

The first session I recall was at Jos's house, his wife running in with platters of tea and out with ashtrays. Meetings took this form: as the initial chit-chat floated away and the air grew opaque with smoke, Sadid or Jos would take the floor, beginning in Spanish, drifting into English, concluding in Spanish.

At issue was a perceived "communication gap" between eivissencs and the foreign community. (The Spaniards, Sadid, Alberto and Marielena, were also "foreigners", in a way, because they were from the peninsula and also, they lived as modern people, not *campesinos*.) Some foreigners took little interest in the people to whom the island really belonged, their history and culture. Of course there were fundamental differences between the two groups. S'Hort wanted to bridge that gap, meld eivissenc heritage and our evolving international ideas, so that there could be, if not a dialogue, exactly, more understanding. For this reason San Miguel was perfect, they said, little more than a ghost town, and so, a place where we might make a contribution and ideally, become part of the community.

We were aiming at an economic gap as well. Even before the Civil War, Ibiza had had a tourist trade. Then, a handful of hotels served Spanish families on vacation and the odd *estranjero*. Now, more and more Europeans were basking on sun beds at the island's new resorts. San Miguel was less than a kilometer away from a development, but the road to the beach bypassed the village. S'Hort hoped to bring those summer tourists into town, and draw residents from around the island in winter.

Certainly business was up at the Bar March where we drank, and at Can Partit where we bought staples and sometimes, one of the chickens running around a cage at the back. Eivissencs were not vegetarians by custom, nor did they patronize boutiques. Yet little by little, they would be won over, was the idea, join us and the regulars in the tea room and restaurant.

Whatever they thought about S'Hort, San Miguel, for the most part, was displaying a good-humored attitude toward the new members of the community. Friendly, but not too inquisitive. That they were watching us, we knew. Most likely, in their usual way, as long as we didn't cause problems they would leave us to get on with it.

Eventually that spring we got down to building. This was equally spontaneous with no overall scheme. People with skills took up corners and created projects. There was a lot of stucco work - built-in benches for the tea drinking areas, corrals transformed into shops. Jim and Sadid shaped delicate arabesques around the bathroom fixtures. Roberta and I gravitated to the wheelbarrow section in a vacant lot across the street. There we could gossip, shoveling dirt through a sieve and hoisting it uphill. She told me Nanni had gone back to Naples for a while. Something to do with aged parents.

One day Jos arrived from Holland and dumped huge crates around the bakery where Franz was teaching us how to mix dough. "Look at these pots," he said, handing out copper saucepans. Cordon Bleu cookware tumbled forth. Corinne looked at me, blue eyes bulging. There must have been half the communal stash in those pots alone. "But ladies," he continued, "here is the pièce de résistance!" He hoisted a box our way. It was a vacuum cleaner, Swiss. The best.

Vacuuming rather than sweeping out a stucco house with tile floors was a novel idea. Even if one owned a Hoover, the houses we lived in didn't have electricity. But what a wonderful machine! We pounced on it and forget about the pans.

Opening night, Jos was squeezing grapefruits into the oven among Franz's cakes. He had served us a trial run of the menu the day before. Most peculiar, his spécialité, I thought. Broiled grapefruit was one of the first things they taught us in cooking class at junior high. There were a few too many garbanzo dishes as well, for my taste. But as we sat down, Sadid raised a glass and said, "Now this is what the island has been looking for." "Bravo!" we all said, and dug in.

Corinne and I were scurrying about with the vacuum. Antonio bathed the boutique in candles and Sadid set out his briefcases and saddlebags on Moroccan rugs. The herb shop wasn't built yet, but two terraces down in the pottery, Jim had installed a wheel and was throwing prototypes.

Some of us appointed ourselves servers and stood at the door. The eivissencs began to file in. Farmers, children, grandmothers - smiling and slightly baffled - filled every inch of the restaurant. They were dressed as for mass, the men in suits, the elderly ladies in their best brocade shawls and kerchiefs, with a pigtail out the back. Most of them sat down to eat. A couple men, habituées of Bar March who joined our late night drinking bouts, ventured down to the tea room. They chatted politely with Bob and drank tea from bowls as if they did it every day.

Bob had constructed a small pavilion in the garden with a

bamboo canopy and shelves full of Chinese teapots. About the time dinner finished and people began filing out there, he announced there would be a surprise. Someone changed the tape on the player. From a dark area below a balcony where people were standing, his girlfriend, a secretarial-looking woman by day, entered and began performing a belly dance. Her hair, let loose from its usual knot, swept across the floor like a broomful of snakes.

Had the people of San Miguel ever seen such things, I wondered? But they were our guests. Courteously they watched and courteously clapped, even the matrons.

Then they left, nearly all at once, with many waves and thank yous, as if the entire evening had been an extended performance. Later, more people arrived, foreign, mostly, drifting from candlelight to shadow as the music changed and the moon floated over the terraces of the tea garden. It was Sunday night.

Next day the sun rose many hours before the proprietors of S'Hort. By the time we arrived it was already siesta. I joined Franz and Corinne cleaning up in the *panaderia*. Alberto paced back and forth, bringing piles of cups from the tearoom, wondering loudly to Marielena where "everyone" was. On Tuesday, S'Hort reopened. A German couple were trying the rissoles. Business in the tea house was a little better than in the restaurant, but the cakes were stale. Franz went to fetch more flour. Alberto, or alternately, Marielena, stood at their post in the boutique watching their children run around the terrace. The place was almost empty.

For two or three weeks we carried on. Then someone called an emergency meeting. It was Sunday morning, and we sat as we had met so many times before, on benches under the fig tree. Only, this time Alberto had the floor. He was not smiling. "Everyone wanted to build this place but no one wants to go to work," he said. "You people think you can turn up for a few hours after the beach and everything will float along.." Etc.

No one said anything. Esprit de corps was wilting like an air mattress in the midday sun.

Alberto was right, in a way. But the problem with S'Hort was more fundamental, to my mind. Our focus had been on the concept, the remodeling and the opening, as if we imagined that once built, the place would generate its own momentum. There were no plans for building clientele or for divvying up the daily tasks. The members had energy and good will, but as facts came to light, very few had expertise, or even experience in business, cooperative or otherwise. What Franz knew of cakes he had learned from his mother in the kitchen. Jos had always *dreamed* of opening a restaurant....and so forth.

The joke was, to carry them forward, most of S'Hort had been counting on the *communal* expertise. So great was our ignorance, commercially speaking, we were just beginning to realize: there was none. Oops!

And Ted? He hadn't been seen since the opening. Rumor was, he had left the island. Called away "on business", someone said.

4

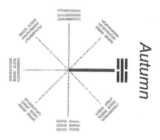

Autumn

Raining in San Mateo

ALL AT ONCE, it was autumn. The wind blew for a week, rustling clouds, threatening, then breaking into a rage. At dawn came the rain. When I lifted the bolt to open one side of the wooden doors, it poured over the threshold onto the cold stone of the *entrada* floor.

I was alone with a two-month-old infant about a mile from a tiny village called San Mateo. For the first couple weeks after Vedra was born, Jim took up his post, pulling buckets of water from the cistern and scrubbing diapers until I could get about. Hating domesticity, he was off after that. Every few days he would ride up from S'Hort on a mobylette with supplies. Nanni was back from Italy and often he came too, wobbling on the back with his belly and wire-framed glasses, like Trotsky from Naples. Nanni always dumped a huge box on the table and began chopping, sniffing, concocting something rich and succulent like squid, while Jim held Vedra.

He was a tall man with huge hands, graceful, balancing his child with command and delicacy between his palm and elbow. The infant was remarkably petite - two and a half kilos, or thereabouts, on the bakery scales at S'Hort. No one had weighed her at the hospital, or perhaps they didn't tell me, angry that we rushed in at dawn when the home birth with Bob went awry. In any case, our Vedra was pronounced sound by Roberta, all parts working and *"Bene, bellissima!"*

Since the winds, neither Jim nor anyone else had come. I was a bit lonely, but not anxious. On the shelves in the entrada, behind a net that kept the mice at bay, sat the stores that got one through an Ibizan winter - a sack of almonds, rice, sausage, dried beans and figs. Next door in the *cocina*, kitchen, a stash of pinecones stood beside the fireplace. Every morning, I would toss big handfuls on for kindling just to smell the resin oozing out the sides. The *cocina* was the only room you could get warm, the place where I stashed my precious tea bags and long-life milk. The cupboard was at least half full.

Camping out in a stone house...well, it was how most of us lived. I rather liked it that way. Even in London, I had been roughing it on a rusty yacht near Kew Bridge. After bathing in a bucket, I would hop on shore, shivering; rush off for the Waterloo train, charge across the Thames on the footbridge, cross Trafalgar Square, and arrive at my desk in the Portrait Gallery, head nearly dry. Invigorating.

Having a house, even one without plumbing, was luxurious by comparison. All spring, Jim and I had searched random roads on the *mobylette*, me pregnant, desperate to find anything. On a tip, we drove up a remote slope and found the landlord, Juan, atop the roof with his son. It was a humble *finca*, one story of tawny-colored stone and earth. A pair of heavy wooden doors flanked by windows either side was all we could see at the front. There would be an *entrada*, entrance and sitting room all in one, and perhaps two small bedrooms at the back. Juan was on top what looked to be the kitchen, a rectangle running perpendicular to everything else, fixing the chimney flue.

The slope the house was clinging to overlooked a magnificent valley of grapevines and fruit trees. Two miles further on, although you couldn't see it, the north coast faced straight into the mistral. In defense, the house turned its back to the wind and the world, and was addressing a hillside of spindly almonds. A passage about ten feet wide had been carved into the slope, as a patio.

There was one distinctive feature: a bread oven, hive-like, glistening in a coat of whitewash beside the kitchen wall. I noticed that the opening where an *abuela* (it was always an old lady) shoved in the loaves was sealed off with bits of cinder block and mortar. The *"tia"* who lived in the house had been dead *"hace tiempo"*, said Juan, not specifying whose aunt she had been. Finally they had time to fix it up. In fact, they were just about to rent it, he said. He smiled, a small, sturdy man with a lovely set of teeth. We smiled back. And that was that.

Eivissencs love babies. A few days after we moved in, Juan came grunting through the door, hoisting an ornately carved double bed. *"Su matrimonial!"* he announced, grinning in the direction of my belly. It was a splendid way to welcome us, and it certainly cheered up the rope-seated chairs and plank tables in the house.

Next, we were admiring a new kitchen floor. In San Miguel, Jim had spotted some workmen ripping black and white marble tiles out of a building. They were happy to get rid of them, helped him hoist load after load on the *mobylette* to bring them to Juan, who was even happier, and laid them, chessboard style, in the *cocina*. The tiles, the raised hearth and chimney hood, the stone walls - it evoked some memory of a fairy tale. Cinderella? Hmm …

When Vedra was born that September, Juan's little daughter, Nieves, appeared with a bouquet. She must have been around seven, short and sturdy like her father, too shy to ask to see the baby. I led her in and she sat down on the bed. Well into the evening, she stayed there, motionless, gazing at Vedra as if it were the Baby Jesus himself lying in the basket. It wasn't her sister or a cousin, or even anyone she knew. What did she see with those eyes, so different from mine at that age?

Eventually, like the magi, she went back home. If Juan had some job to do near the house, Nieves would return, glancing toward the the door, hopeful. On Sunday nights, when people filled the bars and streets of San Miguel, and Jim would bring us in to town, I began to notice eivissencs handling their babies, how whole families would circle round an infant, focused on its every gesture; even teenage boys, holding, cooing at the little person, like a mother.

Apart from Nieves, the stream of friends who came to see our infant had dried up within a month. The thunderstorm was almost a relief when it arrived, something to break the routine. I rather relished the challenge. How many ways can one eat almonds, for instance?

Whenever the rain eased off, I would throw a feed sack over my head and scoot up into the forest looking for something to burn. Not that one needed huge fires at the end of October. The blaze was a friend, crackling, ever-shifting, demanding, warm. Amazing, as well, what it did to something ordinary like beans. Fried over smoldering rosemary, chick peas and garlic in olive oil become, well, *cuisine*, of a sort.

So we settled in, Vedra and I, as for a hibernation, me singing, or rather, bellowing nursery rhymes and ditties, Vedra bouncing along, favoring especially, as it seemed, the weasel that went "Pop!", and "I'm Getting Married in the Morning". Normal tasks using water drawn up from the cistern, in fact anything to do with water, which was practically everything, required a plan of attack.

How long we sat there as one day became another, I don't recall, only the *entrada* festooned in soggy clothes. The storm was gaining ground, angry, pounding holes into the courtyard, casting us adrift from everything but the womb of the house and the spaces my mind roamed whenever Vedra was asleep. Logically, at some point it had to stop. But that seemed further off, harder to envision as time went on. Time behind walls...

I had never been a homebody. At the age when I could walk up to a friend's house and play dolls, I would detour on the way back to an abandoned lot across the street. There was a sand pit, deep and partly overgrown where I hid, and in my seven-year-old imagination it was a raft I was floating on beneath the cliffs. All around was the Mississippi, and I was Huck Finn, taking off.

What is it that one navigates by? After years of study, travel, and some short, but excellent jobs en route to a career, something had told me it was time to have children. I knew nothing about them, yet motherhood seemed right, somehow; the next step. One was ready.

What a shock. At first, I was unsure of every move, except the most instinctual ones, like feeding. Why was she crying when she wasn't hungry? Should I pick her up again? And so forth. Nor had I anticipated the entrapment, inside, alone. Far worse, though, was a new sensation, or rather, an awareness, of plunging so much deeper into life. One was grappling with a new self: stronger, fiercely protective, yes, but at the same time, infinitely vulnerable. How could anyone bear to love this much? It was terrifying.

One night there was a scratch at the door. It was Gypsy, paws covered in mud. I remember letting her in, thinking she had not been away very long, and Gypsy, slinking past, eyeing me as she had been, of late - nervous, guilty-looking, belly full of pups.

Poor half-wild hound. Magical yet, ears twitching at infinitesimal sounds. I had never wanted to tame her. A romantic notion, perhaps, as a friend was always pointing out: "Dogs kill chickens. Face it. If you don't feed her, some farmer is just going to blast her away." I knew nothing of raising chickens; could not envision shooting a dog in recompense.

"She lives off rabbits," I would tell him, adding that she wasn't mine. "Gypsy is a wild animal, living in the woods, not a pet." Even as I tried to express a conviction that she had a right to her own fate, I must have guessed it would never be as simple as that. The land belonged to the eivissencs. One had to accept, if not embrace, their ways.

When I first met Gypsy, our household had its own mutt, a large and friendly half-Alsatian male, very fond of chasing rocks. Before long he was chasing Gypsy as well. I begged the others not to feed her, shooed her away from our place whenever she appeared. In the end, they ignored me. However long Gypsy might evade a farmer's gun, Banjo was bigger, slower, and not at all cunning. The perfect target.

Perhaps my friends were right. Inevitably, she got pregnant and we had a litter of pups in our courtyard. Then one evening, no one returned to feed the dogs until quite late. Gypsy had disappeared. Around lunchtime the next day she surfaced, dragging a baby lamb. She crept off and cowered in a corral after she had laid it in front of the pups, and I had to face what I had already suspected: when you have babies to feed, there is no line between wild game and livestock.

Eventually, the litter was given away. Hardly anyone had wanted a dog. Not long afterward, our household also dispersed. Gypsy followed me to the next house and the next, disappearing for spells, though not as often. Irregularly, and with as much indifference as possible, I fed her. Rice. Somewhere between the lack of money for the vet and spaying, and wanting to believe she was still a free creature, I had allowed nature to follow its course yet again.

What to do? There were too many stray dogs on the island. Following the laws of the people around me, I should kill the pups. Or - coward's way out - let someone else do it.

I fed her that night, brooding all the while, trying to imagine the deed. Did she know what was running through my mind? There was that time - it would have been the early days when she was still quite wild. I was returning after a trip to England. It was dark and I was walking, still quite a distance from the *finca*, when she emerged from the wood to greet me there, as if she knew I was coming, knew I would not want to meet her near the house. Lately I had been discovering uncanny connections with Vedra, how she might be crying in another room, well out of earshot, and somehow I knew it, would rush in to get her.

How could a mother, awakened to an intensity of feeling she had never even imagined, kill another creature's children? Food she must have, but I would make no nest. I was hoping, vaguely, Gypsy would have her pups far away. Meanwhile another voice kept nagging in the background, a thought I had been mulling over for some time. Not taking action is just another type of action.

Some hours later I opened the door. At last the rain was easing off. The sky was brighter than it had been for nights, a faintly glowing moon behind the clouds. Gypsy heard me and came outside. She stood beside me for a while, sniffing the air. Then I went in, and closed the door, and she took off.

Next morning when I opened the door again, the siege was over. Vedra had already been fed and gone back to sleep. Ahh, Peace. I boiled water on a little gas burner, brewed up tea and was walking around the patio with my cup, smelling the damp earth when I heard something in the bread oven. Crawling onto a terrace wall, I crept along to where I could get above the oven and peered down through the smoke hole in the top. It was Gypsy, lying on her side. She looked up at me for a moment and then, exhausted, rested her head. Five bits of life squiggled across her belly, fighting for the milk.

Oh clever creature! She had found the one place I couldn't get at. Too high a space for me to reach down and grab the pups, low enough for her springy legs to jump in and out. She knew.

* * *

That December, 1978, I stepped on a plane with Vedra in a basket, off to visit my family for Christmas. What I didn't know was that we would not return until 1985.

Part II: Then

5

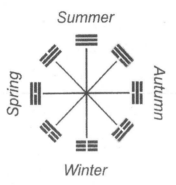

Summer

Autumn

Spring

Winter

San Pedro

TAKING THE LONG view, it seems the most important things in life happen by chance. We never intended to live in the village of San Pedro, for example. For four years, my partner and I had been pounding away at a sort of live-in sculpture on a remote and rainy corner of the United States. Vedra and her new sister, Brigid, slept, played in and worked on it too. In the early 1980s, the frontier spirit was thriving in the Pacific Northwest. Our friends were netting salmon in Alaska, building boats, felling old trees or planting new ones. Duke and I were erecting stone walls and timber-frame octagonal rooms in our what neighbors liked to call a "baronial maisonette". I did not particularly enjoy wielding a staple gun, especially on scaffolding in a snowsuit. I held on, believing we would somehow finish it and leave for that simpler, sunlit life I had known in the Mediterranean on Ibiza.

Sometime around April Fools' Day, 1985, and against all bets in the local tavern, it was finished. We held a massive garage sale and rented the dream. Then a friend stuffed us in her car and took us to the airport. Vedra was six and her sister, Birdie, almost three.

When we finally arrived in Ibiza around June, there were no rooms left at the inn; that is to say, the only offerings had marble bathrooms and swimming pools. Some people still rented old *fincas* with no plumbing, the type that went for $50 a month in the '70s, but mod-cons and more expensive living in general was the trend. It had escaped us, working in the woods.

For a few days we considered moving on to the mainland, where everything was cheaper, people said. Then we ran into Rolph Blakstad, an old friend, a builder who had been established on the island for many years. As it happened, in the process of transforming a client's *finca* into a marble-floored villa, he had just designed a Moroccan pavilion for the garden. Did Duke know anything about architectural follies in wood?

Not long afterward, another friend offered us an apartment he no longer needed in the village of San Pedro. Here was luxury: a bathroom with hot water, even a bidet. The front room had elegant cream-colored tiles with arabesques of brown and grey and a balcony facing the main square; also some rather nice furniture he was intending to leave for an indefinite time. The bedrooms were puny. Still, the rear one led to a terrace overlooking the landlords' garden, and beyond that, fields and hills, so it was a bit like stepping from town into the country out back, especially with the landlord's chickens cluck-clucking down below. The kitchen was the worst part, more closet than room, with one shelf and a tiny window opening onto the next door neighbors' terrace.

What to do? Not the scene I had sketched for my family: an ancient house in the country, with breakfasts under a fig tree, cicadas whirring in the heat. Rather, a second story apartment on the main square of a noisy town I didn't know. We wandered around for the rest of the day. There were two bars and two *tiendas* in San Pedro, a large and ancient-looking church, plus a school and a bank. The town also had a dry goods store and a tobacconist that sold toys and school supplies, along with a pharmacy directly below the apartment. (Vital, I suppose, if one ran out of bandages in the middle of the night?) Convenience was never a selling point with me. We were at least semi-desperate, though. I was feeling resigned and a little depressed.

All day, above the rhythmic hum of Spanish voices, others rose from time to time on the square. They were English, German, or French, mostly, and around sunset they began to gather in the bar called Isla Bonita. Then, one by one, they faded with a jingle of car keys. In the vacuum, new voices filled the paseo: children, taking over the town, it seemed, their parents murmuring in the shadows, some in castellano, some, eivissenc.

It appeared we would be the only foreigners (the first?) actually living within the village. While I had been dreaming of tranquility and the landscape, the reason for dragging the family halfway across the world, I told myself, was to learn about another culture, get close to some of the people. We would all have a better chance at that living in town. Yet we would stick out like odd socks. Tricky, possibly.

From a swallow's point of view, San Pedro is not impressive: a couple streets, some passages and a cluster of whitewashed buildings. It isn't very wide, but the street that cuts the town in half is actually a main road, so that most days at least one large truck will be squeezing through the stream of cars. There is also a cobbled *paseo* known officially as the Plaza de España, although only the postmaster called it that. A row of attached houses with balconies line one side. Mulberries line the other, and on autumn evenings the sun shoots up the street to set their round leaves glittering, like coins.

Our balcony overlooked this patch of stones where children played and people gossiped and cars dozed. On Sunday nights, it became a little more grand when the Andalusians in town came out to promenade, as was their custom, followed by anyone else who felt so inclined.

To get to our door, you had to climb a narrow staircase off the *paseo*. The building we were living in contained the landlords' house as well. Their bedrooms lay across the staircase from us. One step up, another door led to a smaller apartment carved out back next to our kitchen. Everyone shared the staircase, so that, heading out at night, for example, we might pass our neighbor, Piedad, and her husband returning home from work, and the landlord going in downstairs after his evening smoke.

Down on the *paseo*, two large wooden doors marked the official entrance to the landlords' house. It was nearly always bolted. Miguel, his sister Marietta, and his wife, María preferred to enter through the small door just inside the stairwell. Every day at sunrise they left to work on their finca or to help María's parents on theirs. Around one they returned for lunch and siesta. The two women - we called them "Tia (Auntie) María", and "Curly-haired María" - preferred to live in town, they said. Curly-haired María was especially warm, *sympática*; also frail and nervous. I could hear her pacemaker ticking as we talked. She often mentioned it, and the fact that she was only alive *"gracias a Dios"*.

Sometimes we talked farming, how the almond prices were that year, or about modern fertilizers that made tomatoes huge but took away the taste. Whenever I grew wistful about life in the *campo*, both women argued that yes, it was more peaceful there, but it was better for children in town. Even as they kept to themselves and to traditional ways, the women, at least, wanted a different life for Nieves, María's daughter; more modern, interesting, something like what they were seeing outside the door, perhaps.

And indeed, in the 1980s, a lot was happening in San Pedro. There were the women who sat on the steps in front of the tobacconist's, for example. This was Maribel's shop, or rather, domain. It was not much bigger than our bedroom, with children's toys on one side, stationery on the other, a television over the door, and old men at the back, slamming glasses down on a little marble counter beside the till. Rows of magazines with movie stars hung from the doors in front, like flags from other planets.

Maribel was an eivissenc with city ways. At any moment she might be pouring brandy, ogling "Dallas" on the TV, feeding her daughter in the stroller and stuffing pastries in her son's chubby cheeks, meanwhile keeping up with gossip on the steps. She always gave me the cold shoulder, especially when I tried to hold her baby like the other women did. One of them, a squat, well-bosomed woman named Paquita would roll her twinkling eyes as if to say, "What a bitch, that Maribel!" We liked each other right away, and much of what I came to understand about San Pedro I learned sitting on her couch as she sewed dresses for boutiques.

Upstairs from Paqui, as we called her, two lines of wash hung dripping day and night. Ducking under it to go in Paqui's door, you would hear the exotic, guttural tones of Andalusia. José and Anna lived with their five children in an apartment less than half the size of ours. José was a mason. Anna cleaned hotel rooms in resorts on the coast.

Paqui's husband, also called José, worked as a painter. On the nights when they did drink, both Josés went to the bar near Maribel's shop, Bar San Jaime. Their wives stayed home, Paqui churning out frocks while Anna, thin and a bit manic, mopped their stairwell as if she couldn't stop, or perhaps to indicate they were as good as the people she had been cleaning for all day. In San Pedro, both eivissencs and peninsulares clung to to their own sex when socializing. Fiestas were an exception, or when couples went promenading. Then, arm in arm with her man, Paquita only acknowledged me with the faintest nod.

Of course, one key to a community like San Pedro is the bars which, when they are busy, become something like a neighborhood living room. The one near Maribel's, Bar San Jaime, was plain and noisy, with pinball tables and a television. In those days, soaps like "Dynasty" were popular with the women, and children watched the Australian series, "Little House on the Prairie", but only football matches drew large crowds. Most evenings, males under fifteen huddled around a soccer table on the patio, banging and twirling the handles while the smaller children watched, mesmerized, waiting their chance.

Bar San Jaime had a back door onto a passageway right near the *cuartel*. However tiny, San Pedro is an outpost of the Guardia Civil. Peninsulares, all of them, they had brought their families from places like Seville and Valencia, to live in apartments near the lockup. When they drank, the Guardia drank there, in the "Spanish bar", as we called it. One night shortly after we arrived, I came upon a dancing couple in front of Maribel's, teaching Vedra how to do a *pasodoble*. They nodded politely, but when I tried to approach and say something, they vanished. I knew who they were - the mother and uncle of Veronica, a girl who passed in and out of our flat with Vedra's other friends. She had told us her father was a Guardia although I didn't know which one, while the uncle was usually sitting on their doorstep in civvies. Was he part of the *cuartel*, or just living with them, as relatives did in Spain?

I didn't ask. The Guardia Civil, both police and army, were not supposed to fraternize with locals. I certainly wasn't keen on that myself. It struck me they might be wondering what we Yanks were doing there, day after day.

The watering hole preferred by foreigners stood at our end of the street, all whiteness and bougainvillea. From our balcony, you could observe the regulars of La Isla Bonita on the patio, devouring soup of the day, or something called "champagne chicken". Eivissencs also drank there, usually inside at the bar. On Sunday mornings before mass, the handful of tables within the bar were packed with gold-earringed matrons. Late afternoon, the old boys filed in to play cards. Sometimes they showed their hands to Vedra, who peeked over the backs of their chairs, trying to learn what looked like bridge with tarot cards.

At almost any moment, depending on who arrived, the atmosphere inside La Isla Bonita could shift from simple comforts to glamour to intrigue. It became our bar, too.

6

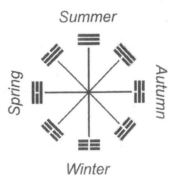

Summer

Autumn

Spring

Winter

The Players

CHOOSING WHICH BAR to patronize in a town with only two sounds awkward, to say the least. The Spanish were quite straightforward about this. In general, people patronized the bar or grocery at the end of town nearest their house, or so they said if you asked them. I suspected at least some of the customers at the Spanish bar were avoiding the foreigners down the street, while the pleasure of drinking next to a Guardia kept expatriates away. Children might appear in either, with or without their parents, but mostly they preferred to be where the action was - on the *paseo*.

If we needed an excuse for frequenting La Isla Bonita, we lived across the street. As if to cover the bases, the girls were often up at the Spanish Bar trying to get a turn at table football. One night Vedra came running back to tell us that little Birdie, who was very good at climbing, had crawled up on a stool and was banging on the bar as if she wanted a drink.

Neither our landlord nor the landladies ever went to a bar. Most evenings, Miguel would stand quietly outside his front door, smoking and observing whatever might be happening while María and Marietta finished the housework. Later, if it was hot and they left the little staircase door ajar, you might glimpse a table lamp in the dark and the *señoras* sitting beside it, hemming handkerchiefs for a few pennies.

I began to notice that some of the eivissencs who frequented La Isla Bonita were also ones who went to church. Was it something to do with the owners, perhaps? I was not sure what to make of Manolo, who served behind the bar. He, and in fact, all his family, who lived upstairs, called everyone *"tú"* rather than the polite *"usted"*, whether they knew them or not. It was their way of nurturing a foreign "scene" - relaxed, intimate, and on occasion, faintly camp.

They also encouraged *cuentas*, or running accounts. One could eat, drink and be merry, like family, for days, weeks even. Manolo would keep track on a scrap of paper behind the bar. I guess most people paid up eventually, but the bar must have got burned now and then, with the number of people passing through in summer. Manolo spoke English, unless you persisted in Spanish, and would sometimes remark, as he leaned back from taking your order, "I feel so *high...*" stretching out the last word, "haaaaiii", as he judged your reaction.

One evening, not long after our arrival in town, I went up to the bar to settle my account. He looked me straight in the eye. "You must be very rich, spending so much money here," he said. Would I take offense, laugh it off, ignore him grandly? I do not remember, but probably I pretended not to notice and pulled out the cash. I was never quite certain whether the face he showed me on any particular day was sardonic, teasing, friendly, or contemptuous. It seemed he was always testing.

Nevertheless, I grew very fond of Manolo, and wanted him to like me, even though I frequently walked out the door wondering whether he had just insulted me and was having a good laugh. Manolo *was* the bar, as his mother, Carmela, was the kitchen, except on Sunday mornings. Then, robed and solemn, he would be in church serving for the priest while Carmela sat nearby on a pew, and his sister Celia filled in for him back at the bar.

On those occasions, Manuel, the paterfamilias, would appear, supervising from a chair. Gold chains dangled from his hairy throat, and sometimes the Moroccan youths who worked his finca sat with him, a little uneasily, it seemed. Manuel did not look especially eivissenc. Some time later when I got to know Carmela, she told me that he had ridden into town on a horse one day and swept her away. Since that must have been years ago, it was possible there some was truth in the tale. I thought it better not to ask.

Just around the corner from La Isla Bonita was Olivia's store, "C'an Bon Profit". It was small, like a country tienda, with pots and mousetraps as well as food, round boxes of salted fish beside the deli counter, and wooden crates of vegetables piled outside. On Sunday mornings she opened for about an hour so that people coming into town for mass could shop. Kerchiefed *abuelas* jammed the doorway. Olivia would be darting from shelf to deli counter next to José, her son. José was about eighteen then, and his job was *bocadillos*, sandwiches, to order. He produced these like a *maestro*, leaning toward you as he asked about the garlic, squishing a tomato on the bread, pouring down a shower of olive oil, joking as he slapped the ham on top.

Like her in-laws at La Isla Bonita, Olivia gave *cuentas*. She kept up a constant patter in Catalan, Spanish or French as she filled the orders and she seemed to be functioning at twice the speed of San Pedro in general, and her husband in particular. In fact, by Ibizan standards Olivia was a city girl. She had left her people, who ran the oldest delicatessen in Santa Eulalia, to marry into a small-town family of churchgoers. Why? And (I was sure I had detected it) why the cold-shoulder act between the tienda and the bar?

Olivia's competition was the supermarket up the street, beneath a row of new apartments. Our next-door neighbors worked behind the butcher counter. Wanting to try something new one morning, I pointed to a lump of beef and ask Piedad what cut it was. Her rough Andalusian voice was difficult to understand. She tried several phrases, then burst into giggles. An Englishman waiting his turn behind me cleared up the matter. "Balls," he whispered.

The stores drew a daily tide of outsiders, in for the morning's shopping, over to the bars, out at siesta when the shops shut. Many were expats who formed their own circles of negotiation and intrigue, which sometimes included us. They had quite different lives from the people in San Pedro and on such a small stage, the more flamboyant among them were a bit of a sideshow. What did my neighbors think of them?

Some expats had good friends among the eivissencs. A handful even learned the dialect. Some clung to their own kind, colonial fashion, and a few treated the local people like servants, but one thing most foreign residents had in common: our legal status. None, officially. During the Franco years when the economy was stagnating, one drifted in without much scrutiny or stamping of passports. The policy appeared to be that provided they spent money and kept out of trouble, *estranjeros* were invisible. Running a business was another matter, requiring a Spanish partner and labyrinthian paperwork if any real money was involved. For the rest of us, the Guardia might harass the odd person, but mostly, they cast a cold but watchful eye.

Then, some time after we arrived in San Pedro, an announcement appeared in the papers. The new Spain of Felipe González was inviting foreigners to come forth and "normalize" their legal status by applying for *residencia*. Several swallowed the bait, but as we suspected, it turned out to be a Kafkaesque process with no foreseeable results. One waited in line with papers and bank statements, and, if lucky enough to reach the desk before closing, there would be a rubber stamp, followed by an instruction to return at such and such a date with another paper and statement. Meanwhile, as before, we were all in limbo, at the discretion of whoever might be in charge. Just who, out at sea on Ibiza, was never clear.

Some days it seemed that everything was in flux. Semis chugged up the main street; convoys of tourists in orange-colored jeeps zoomed through like white noise. The effects of the package holiday and the boom it produced in the late '70s were more visible now. Among the eivissencs, there was a new generation gap. Our landlords were sober, God-fearing people, and in that way, different from most eivissencs I had known in the past, who were not particularly religious, on the whole. Yet like their neighbors, they owned land and were renting a portion of their holdings. Our landladies, who had hardly any schooling, would be sending the daughter, Nieves, to university. Many of her friends would end up moving to the city or working in resorts. When she learned I was writing articles, Nieves said she might try journalism too.

I would not choose a farmer's life myself, but I doubted that the switch to consumer capitalism would bring happiness. In some way, I felt guilty, as an *estranjero*. Could we, who left the modern world to live there, be blamed for a global process that would have happened anyway? Yet we were part of it, even those with spartan ways, part of what was eating up the countryside. Most difficult, for me, was the memory of their generosity in letting us stay.

It was a bit of a tightrope, painful sometimes, living with all these people meeting cheek by jowl. Things that happened and what people said had to be deciphered though many layers - personality, values, culture. By definition, but also how we lived, we belonged to the foreign community. Among them were people I had known for years, a kind of tribal family, and other friends offering work or support. Yet fortune had placed us in a different setting. Even if it were possible, to live apart, in a sort of bubble within San Pedro, was unthinkable. We had to fit in somehow and hope we would be accepted.

Of such aims and predicaments, the girls were blissfully oblivious. Vedra was nearly seven that June we arrived. The night we moved into our apartment, the smaller citizens of San Pedro were on the *paseo* as usual, playing something that looked like tag. When they touched base, a tree trunk near the tobacconist's, they shouted out some phrase. I was watching from the balcony, holding Birdie, wondering how my children would manage in this place, when Vedra ran straight out in her red dress and plastic sandals and hopped into the game.

There must have been about eight children, all somewhere between five and eleven. Vedra ran around among them for a while until she had a chance to try the magic phrase, or rather, something that sounded like it. Contrary to received wisdom, that children in packs are remarkably cruel to newcomers, these *niños* carried on as if she had always been there. By the time their mothers were calling them home, Vedra had perfected the words, *"Aqui no me pillas".* Or, as we would say, Safe.

7

Summer

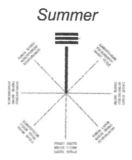

The Scoop

THESE DAYS, SAN Pedro looks the perfect set for a film about a sleepy little town. I suspect that for much of its history it was. Certainly it is a different place from the one whose every orifice was crammed with people, as it was that summer we arrived. For us, coming from a house in the woods, it was like moving into a beehive.

Dawn brought a series of mechanical farts: *putt, putt, whirrrrrrr.* as bicycles propelled by something like hairdryers carried farmers and builders off to work. The owners of these *mobylettes* all parked right below our balcony. Some drowsy time later, La Isla Bonita awoke with a *sweep-scud-sweep* as someone cleaned the terrace, and rearranged the metal chairs. Eventually you would hear voices, and with the reassuring hiss of the espresso machine, the day was officially underway.

Wooden doors creaked open along our row of houses, a few cars trickled in, the doorbell started tinkling in the shop below. From then on, as people and vehicles continued to arrive, the decibels rose with the sun until by midday, the cacophony was as intense as the heat and coming from all directions - laughter in the cafe, babbling on the *paseo*, engines, babies, hissing breaks as trucks crept down the main street.

Then, abruptly, the shops began to shut. People scattered, and by around two o'clock, the heat on the *paseo* had emptied the stage. Now came the adagio, played inside. Behind each door, pots sizzled on the stove. Neighbors began munching their salads, mumbling, yawning, scraping off plates, shuffling off for a lie-down. A great tranquility reigned.

Around four-thirty in the afternoon a car door would slam; engines revved up and down the street, and it all built up again until sunset, when the shops began to shut. In the enveloping calm, notes dispersed toward the shadows, becoming evocative (patter on the patio of La Isla Bonita), or distinct (the thunk-thunking game at the Spanish bar). In the wee hours, one by one, they dissolved. Then peace... a solo, by a dog....more peace.

Within days, Duke announced he was returning to the states, to make money, he said. It was a complete about-face from our idea of leaving everything behind. I didn't argue. One couldn't, with him, if money or work was involved. The pavilion project would not be starting for a while and the travel features I sent to the States were not enough to float the boat. Ibiza was more expensive than we had anticipated. It would not be the first time our family had managed without him. For our final assault on the house he had gone to Alaska, where a young man with a hammer could still earn a nest egg in a few months, while the girls and I turned an acre of mud and rocks into pasture. Our life in San Pedro was luxurious by comparison, rooms we didn't have to build, furniture, a kitchen, well, an alcove, actually, but it had the the basic items. And plumbing.

San Pedro's plumbing had its own rhythms, we discovered. From time to time, with a regularity I never quite deciphered, an odor of chlorine rose from the tap. After a rainstorm it stopped altogether, then returned with bleachy gusto. Did the small genie I imagined crawling up to the top of the tank dump an extra bottle in on those occasions? Taking a bath, one felt like a soaking tea towel. What might it be doing to our stomachs?

So off we went one morning to Olivia's for one large and one small bucket, bright red. We filled the small one with dinner scraps, rehearsing our lines, and down the stairs to the landlords' we tramped, me with the large one, V and B jostling over the small one. We knocked on the door. Curly-haired María opened it and threw up her hands, affecting great delight. *"Qué es esto?"* she said. *"Para el cerdo"*, said Vedra, exactly on cue. For the pig. Brigid, who had only just learned English and was still rather coy, hid behind my skirt while I asked if there was drinking water nearby.

It became our ritual, the first outing of the day. One or both of the *señoras* would appear at the door (Curly-haired María was particularly good at looking surprised) and while I filled our bucket at their cistern, they led the girls out back to feed the pig. That over, the hardest part of the day began, and it filled up the rest of the morning, the laundry. At least I didn't have to pull buckets from the well as we did in the country. In those glorious days (so thoughts would flow with the scrubbing) there was less to do. The water was in an olive grove with views toward the sea. Here, the mind invoked a classical-looking image, something noble like Poussin: Women at the Well. No kneeling on hard tiles beside the bathtub, elbow-deep in suds.

I rejected a scrubbing board, the ultimate badge of drudgery, and lathered more soap on the spots as if to cover them up. It was revenge against my mother, a woman domestically gifted. Whenever she set me cleaning and I pleaded for more soap, she would flash me a huge grin (the word "glee" comes to mind) and say, "all you need, Bonnie, is a bit of elbow grease."

To stay sane (something other than domestic bliss, in my experience), I continued writing articles. Someone local wanted a bit of advertising copy; not something I relished, but he was paying New York prices and the girls needed new shoes. Any other spare moment, I was peering through a lens, trying to shoot like Cartier-Bresson.

For a couple articles I had written in the states, a friend had loaned me her camera to take photographs. Seeing the "shot" was instinctive. Machines were not. Anything mechanical rebelled when I was at the controls. I was overcoming this neurosis with an old Zenit and a new zoom/close-up lens I had found in London. Or rather, Mac found them for me among a jungle of second-hand bits in his dark little shop near Hammersmith Bridge. I knew nothing whatsoever about cameras, but told Mac I was writing for newspapers and wanted to do my own photos. He handed me the Russian camera and a book of instructions, and said it would be the best quality for the money I could possibly find. Then he sold me a Japanese lens. It was so flexible, he said, it would cover all the bases, initially. The camera was cheap. I spent the rest on a sturdy case to house these beasts; a trunk, really, to hide their impossible demands.

I shot about half a roll of black and white for a story about Scottish fishing towns, and finished it in Santa Eulalia where I interviewed a survivor from the Civil War shortly after we arrived. Then I experimented with a couple rolls of color - the children in San Pedro, mostly. Our budget was too tight to shoot and develop much more. I was not into snapshots anyway. One was either concentrating on the act of photography or soaking up an experience with the mind and senses; the two were mutually exclusive, in my book.

Then one afternoon, the stars aligned over San Pedro. Across the street at La Isla Bonita, Bob Geldof and Paula Yates appeared. Geldof had already organized "Live Aid", the first global philanthropic rock concert, and was hiding out before traveling to Ethiopia where he would fight a famine with the profits. With these efforts, he was becoming Media Hero of the Moment. His exhausted body, asleep on the floor of a bush plane, would appear on the front page of the *Guardian* within a month.

Covering the rich and famous had not even occurred to me, yet here was the proverbial big scoop, right in front of my lens. Ibiza was like that - so small, and yet so cosmopolitan, at times. As if to confirm the synchronicity of it all, their daughter Fifi was standing on the *paseo* with Vedra and Brigid, sucking an ice cream. She looked just like them: another brown-bellied child in a bathing suit. I would have an "in".

For the next few days I stalked the quarry. It wasn't difficult, with friends among the inner circle who were escorting them around. I could hardly present myself as a well-known photojournalist, but the real problem was they had come to the island to escape. In San Pedro, for example, they did not often appear together. Bob chose the patio tables of the Spanish bar to avoid the foreign crowd at La Isla Bonita. They went to private parties and hung out at the *finca* where they were staying. Agua Blanca, the nude beach, was de rigueur for the "beautiful people", but they went only once and left early, preferring the quiet coves without crowds.

Meanwhile the girls did their job, unwittingly. They liked Fifi - she had a great topknot of curls, and no doubt it was fun to have another playmate who spoke English on the paseo. I started shooting, tentatively. Just the children, of course. One afternoon I managed to join Bob's table at the Spanish bar. A rather glamorous expat was talking about New Guinea art. He, or a friend, I've forgotten, had bought a few pieces. My brother-in-law had teamed up with an anthropologist at the time and was also collecting in that area. So I slipped into a chair (I had been photographing the children nearby) and squeezed in a few words. Mentioned I'd been doing some articles. Bob said he used to write for the *Georgia Straight*. Did I know it?

I got Bob and Paula's agenda from friends. The day they chose Agua Blanca, the girls and I went too. They played with Fifi and I sat nearby, chatting with her nanny. The trick would be to find the occasion to photograph them. They were asking me about beaches for their last day. I suggested an obscure place near San Carlos where there was only one bar and some fishing boats. They invited us along.

The next day I brought my weapon, loaded with fresh film. The children played. I sunbathed, swam, and visited with the nanny. Vedra and Brigid behaved brilliantly, for some reason; they didn't even mind when Fifi smashed their sand castle. The sun was reaching that perfect late afternoon angle. Paula and Bob were wading and cuddling and smoking near a little jetty where fishermen launched their boats. She was glittering, with platinum hair and a big tattoo. He was standing behind her, a god in sunglasses. My lens saw the cover of *Rolling Stone.*

I strolled over with the camera. There was no point in being coy. It would be either yes or no. " Could I?", I said, holding forth the instrument. Bob groaned slightly. Well, who wouldn't? I don't know, maybe Paula was a generous spirit who saw a mother struggling to make it. She whispered something to Bob. "Okay" he said.

Then the amazing happened. I was just hoping for a shot or two, but they were professionals. If they were doing it, they would take it on properly. So they hugged, and smiled, and turned this way, and then she sat on his lap. I shot like mad. Click, click, click..... clunk! Suddenly the camera jammed. I stammered something about a new camera... Hammersmith. I saw greasy-haired Mac handing me the bargain instrument: "Sure it's the same. The settings are a spot of bother, but you've got more control..."

Geldof reached for the camera and fiddled gently with it. "There", he said, and they posed again. I shot away. Was there any film left? Sometimes it worked, sometimes not.

Afterwards, incredibly, they opened up. Fellow-mates-on-the-job, sort of thing. Gave the journalist their country address and London phone number, and drove off. I began to think about flying to England, meeting them for an interview. My invitation was in the machine, waiting to be developed.

In those days, I kept a diary, writing every day when traveling; otherwise, as the spirit moved. The outcome of this story lies in the empty space between August and September. I got the pictures, or rather, the white strips running across the contact sheets. There was one of Vedra and the nanny in the water, and a funny one of the three girls grinning through layers of ice cream. *Nada más.*

Later, when I got over the shock, I showed the results and the camera to a friend, Rod, who was a professional photographer. I didn't tell him what should have been in the gaps. He peered at me, a bit incredulous. "Lesson number one," he said. "How to load the camera…"

8

Summer

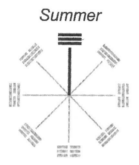

The Birthday Party

To SURVIVE IN a strange place, you have to make at least one good friend. This is where children come in. Paquita and I liked each other right away, but what brought us together was her Marta and my Vedra. They were both nearly seven that summer we arrived, and instant playmates. She also had a daughter a little younger than Brigid named Inés, who appeared every evening on the paseo in an immaculately white dress with ruffles, toddling through the cigarette butts.

Paqui never knocked on my door, perhaps because of the dresses she had to produce every day or because I lived upstairs, so that she could not just pop in on the way to somewhere else, or for some other reason I didn't yet understand. As it happened, her front room opened right onto the *paseo* and I was often passing in search of Vedra or Brigid. She began inviting me in. Before long it was a regular thing, like the women on the steps at Maribel's: Paqui sewing, me sunk into her couch, Inés and Brigid playing around us, and everybody gabbling.

It was wonderfully intimate. The fake leather sofa took up half the room while Paquita and her machine filled the other side. Between us there was just enough space for Marta and Vedra to weave through on their way to the bedroom at the back, and out to the *paseo* again. With the door ajar, as it usually was, Paqui and I were in touch with what was happening outside, as on a balcony, but hidden behind a set of gauzy curtains that covered the entire wall and blew in with the children.

Day and night, the children of San Pedro played on the *paseo*. Everyone more or less kept an eye out. Thanks to all their old or unmarried relatives, the mothers didn't need to hire babysitters in the American fashion, and they seemed to find it a strange idea. When couples did go out together at night, auntie and grandpa often came along. In Eivissa or Santa Eulalia, you would see families strolling the waterfront at two in the morning, children nodding off on their shoulders.

Lacking an army of relatives, and wanting some time as a "person" rather than a parent, I tried to hire our landlady's daughter. Of course Nieves would be happy to watch the girls for an evening, she and María said. When I returned, Nieves refused to take any money.

Maybe she was shy or being polite. It was a new idea, after all. I tried another night, insisting we did that sort of thing in America and I must pay her, as I paid our friend Janan there. Again she refused the money, so I gave up the fantasy of a night out.

At least there was the *paseo*. Public patio, shopping square, parking lot, football pitch, porch, babysitter - what a concept! In the evenings with less cars about, it became one long playground where little people performed deft rituals with their hands, chanting rhymes that might be macabre, like this one:

En la calle-lle,	In the stre-ee-eet,
Venticuatro-tro,	Twenty-four-or-or,
Una vieja-ja,	An old la-a-dy,
Mató un gato-to.	Killed a ca-a-at.
Pobre vieja-ja,	Poor old la-a-dy,
Pobre gato-to,	Poor old ca-a-at,
Pobre punta-ta,	Poor old shoe-oe-oe
Del zapato-to	Tippy-tap-tap-tap.

or downright suggestive:

Soy el Chino capuchino mandarín,
Rín, rín,
De las era verdadera del Japón
Pón-pón.
Mi coleta es de tamano regular
Lar-lar,
Y con ella me divierto sin cesar,
Sar, sar.
Al pasar por un cafetín,
Tín, tín,
Una China me tiró del coletín
Tín, tín
Mira China que no quiero discutir,
Tir, tir
Sol el Chino, capuchino, mandarín,
Rín, rín.

In this one, a Chinaman is talking about his pigtail (of a normal size, he tells us) with which he "never ceases to entertain himself". Passing by a cafe, he attracts a girl and she pulls it. He tells her he doesn't want to argue, for he is a mandarin. He is also *capuchino*, "hooded", like a Capuchin friar. Which makes you wonder...

One rhyme they sang a lot went round and round the zodiac, *"Cap-ri-cor-nio, Le-o, Can-cer, Ari-es, Li-bra, Pis-cis, Tau-ro.."* while they faced each other, slapping hands with the rhythm: same ones; diagonal pairs; palms up hitting palms down, and so forth. Then a new game appeared one day. For this you had to save a remarkable number of rubber bands and knot them together into a loop. This you strung around two chairs and then hopped back and forth in the middle, entangling your ankles in complicated patterns, like Cat's Cradle. It was called "French skipping" and whether or not it came from France nobody knew, but it kept them tied up in the most ingenious knots.

By September, I was wondering what to do about Vedra's birthday. She now had two sets of playmates, the San Pedro gang, and the children of my longtime friends, who all lived some distance away. It seemed a great idea to have a birthday party in the village. Fun for them, and possibly for me, an opener. Most of the mothers and I had not got beyond the level of *"Hola"*. Now there might be something to talk about and possibly (here their immaculate floors glimpsed through doorways made me uneasy) they would even attend? There would have to be another party with my friends and their children, though. It would be too awkward in the small space of our apartment with two groups who didn't know each other, especially with them speaking different languages most of the time.

This was sheer masochism on my part. The girls' birthdays had always been a private purgatory. Once the parties started, excitement carried me along, but for days before I writhed in anxiety - would the event live up to expectations? Apparently, I thought it a success, for I recorded it in my journal (disasters got less press, on the whole):

September 3   Vedra's 7th Birthday 1985

We invite an untold number of kids from the village. I am in a panic - will the cake come out, will the house be clean enough, will enough kids come?

Grandma and Grandpa call in what appears to be the middle of the night.

The time arrives. Fortunately lots of them show up. The atmosphere is something like a football game - every now and then they all burst into another chorus of *"Cumpleaños Feliz"*. We play pin-the-tail-on-the-donkey and pass-the-parcel. It is a huge success. They don't know the games but they love them. Patricia wins the football.

Fortunately they all leave in time so I can mop up for about the seventh time in the last twenty-four hours. Chocolate cake everywhere. I am so sick of the stuff I can hardly look at it.

We shoot for the second party on Agua Blanca. I leave the keys locked in the apartment for the hundredth time. Fortunately Piedad is across the street in the bar. Then the car won't start. Vedra and I try to push it. At last a gentleman comes to our aid.

At Agua Blanca, finally, we can all breathe a sigh of relief. The kids are all in the water. I have a pizza from Isla Bonita to stuff them with, and the adults have a bottle of Smirnoff...

I barely knew Piedad next door but she was getting to know us, thanks to my habit of locking us out. In our small town in the states, people left their doors open. I wasn't used to carrying house keys. Not that San Pedro had any crime to worry about, but our apartment door locked automatically with a snap just as the brain was saying "oops - keys!" The remedy was to crawl over the railing from Piedad's terrace onto ours, and in our back door.

Piedad had a daughter, Sonia, around Vedra's age. A couple times we had offered to take Sonia with us to the beach. Piedad was most emphatic. Her husband didn't want Sonja to get sunburned, she said. I began to suspect their real fear was the scatter-brained *gringa*, who might forget their daughter, like the keys.

As it happened, Sonia was next in line with a birthday party. A few days before, passing Piedad on the stairs, I told her my girls were excited about it. "You must come too," she said. "At our *cumpleaños*, everybody is invited." It seemed (was it just my imagination?) she emphasized the "everybody". Hmm…

Their apartment was narrow and dark, squeezed into the back of the building, much smaller than ours. On the night of the party, it was crammed with people, especially peninsulares like them. In the middle of the room was a long table covered in chips and crackers and drinks which almost everyone was ignoring. The parents drank a little and played sometimes with the children, who ran in and out singing *"Cumpleaños Feliz"* from time to time. There were no presents. Piedad and her husband, whose name I've forgotten, beamed, triumphant. Both of them worked behind the butcher's counter in the supermarket. They didn't appear to be well off. They must have gone to considerable expense.

The next day, Maribel's son, Vicente, was in our place, waiting for Vedra. We talked about the birthday parties, and then I asked him if they ever played games like we did at Vedra's party. *"No,"* he said, looking puzzled. Did he like the games? *"Sí"*. And that was that.

Later I spied Piedad opening the door of her apartment. Boldly, I put the same question to her. "Oh no," she said. "We don't do that." And in a roundabout way, she began to explain that in their view, giving a prize to only one child was unthinkable. Parties were for everybody.

I had never thought about it. Those innocent American games we grew up with - "Pin the Tail on the Donkey", "Musical Chairs", "Pass the Parcel". We were competitive to the core.

The Yank retreated from society for several days.

9

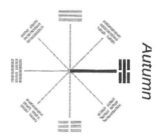

Autumn

"Cole"

ONE MORNING WHEN I was sitting on Paquita's couch watching her sew, she asked me why I wanted to live in Spain. We had been talking about the *residencia* permits and how difficult it was to get one and whether the government really intended to issue them at all. Perhaps she was wondering why we had abandoned a more comfortable life in the states. After all, we owned a house, even if we had to build it ourselves.

Their lifestyle was humble, at best. With Paqui sewing dresses until around nine at night and José working as a laborer and painter, they managed to afford a tiny apartment with two small bedrooms. Except for the front room, where there were windows on the *paseo* side, the other rooms were sections of a dark passage that led to a patch of weeds out back. Here Paqui kept her washing machine. She demonstrated it to me in her proud, positive way. The "machine" had a small cylinder like the ones in electric models, only you cranked it by hand. You also did the plumbing, pouring in the water by the bucketful. I had no washing machine at all, but compared with their apartment, ours was quite grand and light, well-aired with high ceilings; of another class altogether. And I had something she longed to acquire, a driver's license.

I wondered about them, too. While he appeared to be friendly, José was hard of hearing and said little when I was around. He shouted mostly, and his voice was rough; the ends of words stayed back in his throat, trapped, Andalusian style. His style was fairly crude as well - in the door, *"Hola"*, out again. Was it the sight of women gossiping that sent him out the door, or the awkwardness of speaking to someone learning the language, and different, in fact, altogether unknown? Paquita spoke clearly, correcting my grammar as if she were my tutor. She was ambitious too; wanted Marta and Inés to learn English. Knowing that her family came from the outskirts of Barcelona, I wondered why she never spoke their provincial language, Catalan, even to eivissencs.

Language was a prickly issue once again. The name of our town and others had been crossed out on the road signs and the Catalan name painted in. Since Franco's death, some Catalans had been pushing for a separate state, using their language like a flag.

Nothing new, really. Barcelona and Madrid had been at odds since the marriage of Ferdinand and Isabel, when wars directed from Madrid were fueled with tax from Cataluña, a province of wealthy merchants. Like salt to the wounds, at the discovery of the New World, Isabel denied Cataluña its share of the trade. Over time, the ever-industrious Catalans had prevailed, economically at least. By the 1980's, Catalan was being taught in the schools, in Ibiza as well as on the peninsula.

When I mentioned that San Miguel was now Sant Miquel to Paquita, she paused for a moment and then announced, as if to the children as well, "There is only one Spanish language: castellano." Was she against the separatist movement, then? As we grew close and my castellano improved, I tried to find out. Inevitably she would steer the conversation toward chitchat. Maybe she wasn't interested in politics, or maybe it was too sensitive a topic. On the island of Ibiza, they as well as we were outsiders.

I was beginning to realize that however small and Spanish it had remained, San Pedro was a complex community, evolving at that moment. Even among the eivissencs, some were living a semi-medieval life, like our landlords, while others acquired bits and pieces of the modern world, like Maribel, watching "Dynasty" in an electric-blue sweater and black stretch pants. Then there was Olivia, traditional in form, but outward-looking, with her French and her international recipes.

Olivia kept to her tienda as fiercely as our landlords clung to their house. She was an energetic, independent spirit and I liked her immensely, especially the way she ignored her mother-in-law who sat every day in a kerchief and shawl, scowling from a chair at the bottom of the shop. Anyone wandering toward the cooking pot and notebook section would feel the *abuela's* eyes like a needle. She disapproved of customers finding things for themselves in the modern fashion, as if they were bound to be shoplifting. Nor did she approve of Olivia, apparently. The feeling was mutual as far as I could tell.

Bored with cooking, I pleaded for a recipe one morning. Olivia motioned for me to come round the cheese counter and we escaped the *abuela's* eyes through a door leading to the sanctity of her kitchen. She regarded me across a number of immaculate tiled surfaces, and drawing herself up like Julia Child, pronounced, "Cuisine is very simple. Just make some rice…" (lifting a lid on her stove and stirring the contents) "and when it's almost cooked, add some of this cod" (she tossed me a package of fish from her freezer) "and some tomatoes and parsley. Voilà!" She even suggested we go for coffee sometime, but I thought it unlikely since Olivia never left her shop.

I felt honored. Only once had Paquita invited me into her kitchen although we sat nearly every day in her front room. On that occasion she was demonstrating how to make a Spanish tortilla, an omelette with onion and potatoes. The trick involved putting a plate on top the frying pan and flipping it over to turn the tortilla. More than the cooking lesson, I was noting how immaculate her kitchen looked. In the middle of making dinner, every dish and surface was gleaming except for the pan and the plate she was using at that moment.

The more I got to know people like Olivia and Paquita, the more awkward I began to feel. Because of the language barrier, or because they lived such different realities, or for any number of reasons, certain foreigners ignored the local population as much as possible. Occasionally, with Paqui on the *paseo*, for instance, an acquaintance would stroll up and begin talking to me as if Paquita didn't exist. And then, as in any community, beyond the happy encounters of a normal day there are certain people who are avoiding other people. We were only beginning to know our neighbors, around a hundred residents. San Pedro was such a small stage, anyone stepping onto the *paseo* was in the spotlight, so to speak. What gaffe might one be committing?

At least I fell into a well-defined and popular category in Spain, Mothers of Small Children. These women had different methods, though. Some were painfully familiar.

My mother looked terrific in her hat and gloves, but to get there she had to put in several hours grinding the ringer of her washing machine and ironing. Then she would polish our shoes, curl our hair, put us in matching outfits, and parade her three girls down the street to where my father worked. How I hated sitting still in front of the mirror, a hideous curl winding its way around my head like a sausage.

Even if I had wanted to play with my children's hair, which I didn't, there had been little time for that in America between hammering up the ceiling and installing the sink. Once a week or so one went to the laundromat. Now I was washing by hand in a place where people judged how much you loved your children by how they looked. Our flat appeared to be the penthouse of an anthill, so one was also mopping several times a day. More and more, to my horror, I was becoming the 'fifties housewife, drowning in the tedium of broom and bucket, mouth echoing commands to not get their dresses dirty, to come into the house....

September arrived and with it, everyone was talking *"cole"*. The *colegio*, primary school, stood at one corner of town off a side street. Children entered the nursery at four and left for the secondary school in Eivissa at fourteen. They came from around the district, little shepherds from the country as well as future hoteliers from the coast, plus the San Pedro tribe. The school had a good reputation. What that was based on I didn't know, but before long Vedra was talking *"cole"* like everyone else.

What to do? Most foreigners we knew sent their children to "Mary's school", where I had taught in the '70s. It was Mary who had made it possible for me to stay on the island. Her school was some distance away and quite expensive. But good. We were becoming part of San Pedro, though. If Vedra went to the English school, it would mark her as an outsider again.

In 1966, I had gone to France for a semester at the University of Grenoble. It was my first time outside the United States and, a greenhorn from the Midwest, I was dragging three suitcases of clothes and beauty products.

At the apartment with student housing, the one bedroom was

already occupied by a French girl. The landlady showed me her own accommodation (a camp bed in the kitchen), and indicated I would be using something similar in the hallway. The bathroom was as bright as a coal pit and full of dripping laundry, but apparently one wouldn't be using it much anyway. "One bath per week", said Madame des Francs.

The French girl, whose name I've forgotten, was also at the University. That evening she invited me in for a *tête-à-tête*. We were chatting away, well, she was, and I was straining to understand, when at some point I got in a word about clothes. What might the fashionable French woman wear to class? She opened her closet. Hanging on the rail was one navy jacket and matching skirt, and one blouse. In the emptiness around them, I saw myself for the first time: a pampered, middle-class, oh-so-innocent American.

For some of us, bumping up against the "foreign" is when the mind awakes, and we become most intensely alive. I wanted my children to have that opportunity as early as possible. The best solution would be to enrol Vedra in the village school. But would they let her in? I didn't have my *residencia* yet, for example. What Pandora's box would that open? Nevertheless, we spread the word that Vedra would like to attend San Pedro school, hoping someone - the mothers of San Pedro maybe? - would stand behind us. With V, one had stay enthusiastic on the one hand, while preparing her for the possibility that she might end up at Mary's school.

On the morning in question, we awake with ridiculous amounts of time to present ourselves tubbed and scrubbed before the dragon who will decide Vedra's fate. Dragon she must be, judging by the way Paqui utters the words, *"la Directora"*, Headmistress. It is raining for the first time since we came to San Pedro.

La Directora arrives and calls us in. She is younger that I expected; quite good-looking (no obvious spikes) but tailored, a trifle too polite. In fact, abrupt. She would put this foreign woman precisely in her place, it is clear. She directs us to return at 1:15 p.m. with some official documents from the *ayuntamiento*, city hall, which must be approved before V might be admitted. La Directora is parading her diction like lace to my ragtag castellano. I think she's using a lot of the conditional and the subjunctive too. Not a good sign.

V and I sneak off like truants for a drink at the bar. I am trying to sound optimistic even as I make encouraging noises about what we'll do if... V is wonderfully upbeat. Perhaps she doesn't grasp the situation, or really doesn't care what school she goes to. Manolo hands her an enormous croissant, I order a coffee, and staring out at the rain, we contemplate the life academic: school supplies, who might be in what class, teachers one has heard of, and so forth.

Meanwhile I am grilling myself. Why didn't I think to bring a document from her previous school? What kind of a parent am I, anyway? Later we go around the corner and join the lineup at the *ayuntamiento*. They smile indulgently at the sight of a mother and child and give us a thick, long, and very grand piece of paper that simply states we "live at the house of..." Someone has been a little too fastidious, however. At the top is a stamp that says "Provisional".

We return to the Directora's lair, handing the document to a secretary, and sit down to wait. In a little while she calls us in. She is smiling now for some unknown reason; almost warm. She ignores the "Provisional" stamp and says nothing about the missing paperwork from Vedra's school. All is bright and beautiful, at least in this corner of the world, and V starts tomorrow. (What did the *señora* have for lunch, I wonder?)

Off we go to the bar again to celebrate. Vedra, and it would seem, our family are "in". Across the street, Birdie appears at our balcony window half-naked, dazed and bedraggled from her nap. She peers out through the rain, no doubt wondering where everyone is. Full of good fortune, we cannot stop laughing at the public display of her grubby face.

10

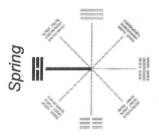

Spring

Pep the Shepherd

IT WAS SPRINGTIME, early in March, and two friends were sleeping under our dining table. Back in the '70s when people were leaving cities like London to raise goats or poach salmon, they had bought an abandoned school in Wales and transformed it into a small factory. There among the sheep farmers, David and Jacquie turned out aerodynamic chairs and origami hats, applying tricks they had learned at the Royal College of Art.

We had made the pilgrimage to their workshop with gothic windows and tossed sticks from all the village bridges. Now they had come to see us with their toddler, Kate, and even though Duke was away for a few months, we were six people, crammed into the apartment. No one cared. The weather was glorious. It was still too cold for swimming, though, so out came the maps, and talk of hikes.

One morning, we drove toward the *finca* where I lived in the early days, the one near Jaime's orchard. We left the car at the edge of a pine forest and began following a track downhill. Halfway there, little Kate struggling with the brush, we climbed onto a wall and crossed a terrace to a dirt road. For a moment I was lost. An alien wall of concrete was blocking off what appeared to be a new vineyard. The vineyard was relatively large, for Ibiza. So were the gate and wall. Wedged into the ancient network surrounding it, the thing looked like a tumor.

David and I loved a good debate. Agreed, the thing looked monstrous, so we considered it from an economic point of view. He opened (he usually did) by calculating the investment required and possible profits for a small vineyard, tossing the ball in my court with:

"Let's say, Bonneville, we each put in a thousand..."

"Just wait till you taste the stuff, my darling," I said. "It's what you and I would call a lusty brew. It would never sell, except maybe in a *restaurante tipico*."

"Ahhhhhh, most likely that's because they can't be bothered to age it...."

And so forth, on down the hill.

At the bottom where the walls ended, three eivissencs were standing under a trellis in front of a small house. They looked distinctly jovial. As it happened, they were sampling wine from the very vineyard we had been discussing. Would we like to try some?

Off they went for more glasses and lemonade for the children. We gulped the vino. It was rough and tasted rather like the blackberry wine I used to brew on our kitchen counters in the states, but the sun was hitting the zenith, the grape was powerful, and within a glass or two we were all entwined.

In our epicenter stood a slightly grubby character named Pep, booming through a vast grey beard. His voice shook tufts of curls, held down like spaniel ears by a cap, his eyes mere glints beneath the brim. He was a shepherd, we discovered; in fact, he lived not far from my old *finca*. He didn't recognize me, and I felt sure I had never seen him, although he had been invited in for a drink at our house, he said. Much later as we were leaving, he mentioned there was a *casita* for rent at the edge of the *huerto*, just below the spring.

A few days after David and Jacquie left I went to see it. The *casita* belonged to our old neighbors who owned the *huerto* and lived on top of the hill. Jaime senior was long dead, but his son Jaime was still working the finca with his mother, Eulalia. It was he who had cemented the floor of a large corral and roofed it with *vigas*, juniper beams, like a traditional house. There were two rooms - one for food and the inevitable flies, I reckoned. Jaime was showing me the other, the combination living and bedroom, about ten by fifteen feet.

The *casita*, as they called it, was, in fact, a gentrified sheep shed, but at least there was a little patio in front, and I loved the trough of water running alongside it, the way it was feeding the oleander and the grapevine. Maybe some geraniums…

The old yearning for a house in the country - it would not go away. San Juan seemed to have everything. School, cafés, grocery stores, and a community we were beginning to know. In contemplative moods, though, it was the *campo* I yearned for, poking my nose into ruins whenever we hiked out of town, admiring the thick, hand-shaped walls, dark and tranquil *entradas* with odd steps leading up to mysterious rooms.

Jaime's "casita" had no architectural charm whatsoever, except for romantics like me who prefer unrendered stone walls to tidy ones made with cement blocks. True, they were too thin to keep out the heat. But the place cost less than a hundred dollars a month. We could just afford to rent it through the summer and still hold onto the apartment.

In the end, it was the land that seduced me. Old Jaime's *huerto* was a short walk away. I remembered the white chamber of the spring glowing in the moonlight as I crept through the garden eating cherries. No doubt that is why, our first night in the new house, I promised the girls an excursion to my secret place.

We had been playing house all day. First we made furniture Shelves: throw ropes over the ceiling beams and knot them around a tier of boards at both ends. Closet: more ropes, then a bamboo pole for hanging clothes, suspended between them. Chest of drawers? Toss your socks and oddments into baskets.

We munched sandwiches, admiring our work, then hiked down to a *tienda* to buy a ladle and some buckets. For the kitchen, Jaime had given us one bench, a table and chairs, and a stove out on the patio under a small roof. We created the rest. Plumbing: a bucket for spring water on the table, covered with a pot lid. Two other buckets (one for washing, one, rinsing) set on a bench, as the sink. For a drying rack, the rest of the bench. Last, I waved my magic wand and presented our new toilet: a roll of paper on the windowsill, a garden hoe on the patio, and any distant spot.

At some point as we were finishing, Eulalia appeared in the doorway. She must have been near sixty then. Years of farming had weathered her face; her body was the same, erect and robust. Politely, she refused the invitation to come in. Then, rather formally, she kissed me on both cheeks, piercing me with such a straightforward gaze, I felt quite humbled taking her gift. It was a simple basket of tomatoes, offered as if it were so much more than food, with a dignity of bearing that was her trademark. Rectitude enveloped Eulalia, even when she was feeding chickens in the cactus.

That night, full of eggs and Eulalia's tomatoes, we set off, stumbling through the brush behind the *casita* toward a path leading uphill. Happily, the moon was nearly full and rising behind us, like a lantern. As we reached the top, I spotted the trail I was looking for. Well-worn by centuries of water carriers, it clung to a stone wall that crossed the slope and turned downhill at the spring.

We followed it all the way and were just rounding the corner by the spring, chattering, kicking up pebbles, when, from somewhere deep inside the chamber, a troll spoke. Vedra and I jumped. Birdie swung around and clutched my legs. *"Buenas noches,"* boomed the voice. *"Buenas noches,"* I said, trying to sound as nonchalant as possible, for the girls' sake.

It was Pep, unmistakably drunk, wallowing in the fright he was giving us. He emerged from the spring, jug in one hand, staggering. *"A dónde vas?"* "Where are you going?" The words rolled around his mouth, hissed out the lips.

I mumbled something, finished with a definitive *adiós* and, grabbing the girls' hands, turned toward the house as if the conversation were now concluded. The voice rose in pitch. Didn't I like the *casita?* Wasn't it he, Pep, who had told me about it? And so on. He must accompany us home, he said.

All I could think to do was ignore his innuendos and carry on politely while I worked on a better idea. The *casita* was not far away. We headed firmly in that direction. Pep followed.

As we got closer, I scanned the terrace - where on earth had I left the hoe with the hammer head? Mercifully, when we arrived at the wall alongside the patio and I declined to "show him the house", as he put it, he stumbled off.

For the next fifteen minutes or so, I fumbled madly with the bits of metalwork that were supposed to lock the door. At least I had located the hoe. Before long, Vedra had to make a trip to the "toilet". I grabbed the weapon and we braved the dark. As I feared, there was the glow of a cigarette up on the hill, maybe a hundred meters away. As soon as Vedra finished, I backed into the doorway and stood there in the light, weapon in hand, waiting.

At long last he laughed. A rollicking bellyful. Then, muttering something about a jug at the spring, he vanished.

Next day Pep stayed away, but not far enough. All afternoon his voice enveloped us, bellowing orders to his sheepdog, Celia, from a field near his house. Sunday morning a different Pep appeared at our patio: scrubbed face; dirty hair neatly combed and tidied under a new cap; clean, yes clean trousers. Polite as could be, he explained that he was on his way to buy bread from Eulalia, and would we like some. "No. Thank you," I said, ushering the children inside and shutting the door.

That afternoon I walked up the hill and across Eulalia's courtyard of flowerpots to knock on her door. After the customary drink (chamomile tea, on this occasion), I asked her what to do. Were we safe, with Pep around? Perhaps Jaime, now the "man of the house", could speak to him, and so on.

Eulalia laughed, with more than the usual gusto, it seemed to me. "Señora," she said, "you have nothing to fear from this man. He is harmless, *nada*, so long as you" (here she straightened her spine and peered, it seemed, into the depths of my soul) "make it absolutely clear where you stand."

Whether it was Eulalia and Jaime or my new "clarity" that conveyed the message, within a few days, the sheep grazing suddenly improved on the other side of the valley. We could have ignored Pep after that. Except that, apart from Jaime and Eulalia, Pep was our nearest neighbor, the only eivissenc for some distance. Why live there if we couldn't interact with them, like strangers in a bubble? Eulalia seemed to be saying that Pep respected certain rules even though he was uncouth, from my point of view, anyway. What sort of person was he, behind the macho bluster?

Eventually, we established a protocol. When the girls and I saw him in the fields on our walks, we would say hello and talk. If we were anywhere near his house, Pep would invite us in for a drink. He gave the girls Coke and made instant coffee with lots of sugar for us. We would joke with the kids or talk about how certain crops were doing, or about people we knew, or changes in the valley.

At some point in the conversation, and rather blatantly, his hand might reach over toward my knee, for instance. I would slap it sharply, and carry on talking as if nothing had happened. Or he would drift into a flood of eivissenc I couldn't understand, rolling his eyes the while. I would pretend not to notice and talk directly to the children. After a pause, the conversation resumed.

It was posturing, a kind of dance, and by now faintly ridiculous, yet we carried on, as if it were his duty to make these approaches, and mine to ignore them. He never again came anywhere near the *casita*.

Late in July, the nights suffocating with mosquitoes and heat, Pep invited us for *paella*. It would be a full meal, a great honor, considering his poverty, and we had to go. Pep's house was two small rooms of rough stone with an earthen floor that smelled of damp bird droppings. Understandable, considering the bits of seaweed falling through the roof slats and his flock of palomas, doves, circling overhead. With the heat, though, more flies were invading his dark entrada, crawling on the bacon suspended from the ceiling. At least the food would be boiled...

Towards noon on the day of the feast, I sent the girls off with their friend Patricia - our advance flank, you might say. Presumably, that would set him cooking while they played with Celia outside. About an hour later I grabbed my straw hat and stepped into the heat. At that point it was reasonable to assume that by the time I arrived the *paella* would be nearly ready. Like civilized people, we would visit for a little while, the children and I could lay the plates, and we'd all sit down to eat.

But no. A short distance before Pep's house, I came upon Vedra, hiding behind the giant leaves of an agave, sobbing. Before I could reach her to ask what was wrong, Patricia and Birdie ran up and announced that Vedra was crying because Pep was killing birds.

Poor child! Why hadn't I thought of it? For the eivissencs, *paella* was not so much an everyday meal as a communal dish for celebrations. In the restaurant, which is where we ate it, enormous pans of fish on saffron-colored rice arrived with some ceremony, usually to a large group. At the beach, families made *paella* over a fire, heaping on the day's catch. In the *campo*, where the catch was flesh, not fish, that must mean: first you kill it. Together. Then then you cook it. Together.

The idea of cleaning and gutting a bird (something one really should learn, but not in this heat, please) in Pep's fly-ridden cavern was too much. I drifted in and out, gulping air, while Patricia and Birdie helped him with the plucking. Perhaps because they were so young, only six and four, it seemed more like a game. Vedra peeked in the door from time to time, sniffling.

I had watched my father kill birds once. On that occasion, instead of hunting pheasants he was shooting pigeons for target practice on my grandfather's farm. I must have been about Vedra's age and I remember how he twisted their necks if they didn't die instantly. It seemed horrible, yet I knew that he was not a cruel man.

Pep had killed both a chicken and a dove to feed us, no small sacrifice for him. Our family ate very little meat but I couldn't say we were true vegetarians. At least, not yet. And somewhere in the back of my mind was a code as ancient as the Greeks, perhaps as old as travel, because it makes it possible: the law of host and guest. The host supplies protection and what is needed. The guest accepts the offerings with good grace.

I held my breath and, looking away, reached toward the bowl with the birds. Petal-soft feathers, easy to pull, came off in my hands. No bugs, no grit. Of course! He had put boiling water on them, like in the instructions - where did I read that - *Larousse Gastronomique?*

After much chopping and sautéing and waiting, when it was finally cooked, I suggested we carry the table outside and dine in the fresh air under a fig tree. Pep seemed to like the idea, the woman's touch, perhaps, or maybe the ceremony it gave to the occasion. There were strange bits - lungs or innards? - succulent, unlike anything I'd tasted before. Ahh... the paloma, I was thinking, and probably the freshness of the meat. I had never eaten it straight from the animal like that.

We sat there, safe from the heat under the arms of that giant fig, enveloped in its milky scent, and I remember leaning back for a rest and seeing Pep across the table, grinning, triumphant, bits of chicken sticking out the sides of his mouth. He was watching the kids gobbling up the *paella* as if it were their favorite pizza. Even Vedra.

I I

Winter

Matanza

IT WAS THE almond blossoms I saw first, running onto the balcony. Pink, paper-thin, they framed the dying pig with the same indifference they showed winter's wind and rain. He might have been a lovely stone or hillock.

It had begun just as the day's first cup of tea was sliding down my throat: the nerve-curdling squeals. No one had warned us. Nor had I ever witnessed a *matanza*, yet even before I looked down into the landlord's garden, I grasped what was happening.

We knew this pig. It was Miguel and María and Marietta's, but ours too, in a way. Didn't Vedra and Brigid tramp down the stairs every morning with their bucket of scraps? Usually it was María who answered the door and led them through the darkness of her kitchen to the garden where he would be grunting and snuffling in his stall. On very cold mornings she cooked a sort of gruel out there with potatoes that were too small, wheat husks, old fava beans and the like, and shoved it in with the scraps while the girls watched. Was there some hint in recent days, some detachment in her voice that I had missed?

Thank heaven the girls were away for the day. He lay, twitching on a wooden table, the men holding his legs while the women rushed forth with bowls, catching his blood. It spurted onto their aprons and up their arms.

His suffering was unbearable. I went back inside and shut the door, as if to blot it out. Yet how could I? My own father had butchered cattle; learned how to do it on his father's farm. Growing up, I ate it every day - bacon for breakfast, baloney for lunch, chops for dinner, roast on Sundays. Never mind what one served to one's family. My own cells, grown from butchered animals.

I went back out and peered over the railing. He was dead now, mercifully. One of the men was running a blowtorch over his body, singing the hairs and scraping them off. How odd in the midst of this primitive ritual, the blowtorch. The smell drifted up on the damp air, and I remembered my mother shoving a turkey into the flames on the stove to remove stumps of feathers my father had missed.

A while later I threw on a sweater and went down to the garden. Two ladies I didn't recognize, probably María's relatives who lived near Eivissa, were sloshing something around in huge bowls with sticks. It was the stomach and the long tubes of his intestines. They turned them inside out and ladled boiling water over them with a gourd. Casings for the sausage, they said.

On the way to becoming sausage, his guts were to have a long series of ablutions, and as the women handled them, they began to glow, like a freshly washed face. First, salt: three scrubbings and rinsings, off to the side, on a stone. Then soap (an ordinary laundry bar, I noticed) - three more scrubbings. Next, one of the women squeezed oranges and lemons into the lot, and started mixing and rinsing that. Six times, she told me. Meanwhile the other lady removed the stomach lining with a knife and plopped it back in with the rest for the finale: three more dousings, with vinegar.

The woman with the knife turned out to be María's sister, Margarita. I watched her sturdy fingers, red at the tips, wondering how old she was. Forty, fifty maybe? Difficult to tell at a glance. While their brothers went to school, these women were kept at home from about age twelve to work on the *finca*. They had been toiling ever since, outdoors, indoors, Sundays. Even in December, when for a period Miguel appeared some afternoons on the *paseo* with a "harvest in, I'm on holiday" look on his face, his sister and wife were inside at it.

The women were wearing what they always had on: broad-brimmed straw hats and what my grandmother called a "housedress", a knee-length printed cotton thing that buttoned up the front. Grandma wore one too until she died, whether digging in her flower bed or cooking, or playing canasta with her sisters. Only for church she put on a nicer dress, as they did, and wore a Sunday hat.

Like most country eivissenques, these ladies wore no makeup or adornments other than small gold earrings; no hint of contemporary hairdos or fashions. As far as one could tell, they had little interaction with women of the modern urban type, and even if they were interested in exploring what being a "woman" in that sense might involve, what opportunity did they have to try it out? And would they, given the choice?

They were telling me about school, how they regretted leaving it, and their relative ignorance. I imagined them wanting more freedom, leisure, like the foreign women they saw in town. *"Muy elegante"* was a phrase they used for some who were well-dressed, and there was a certain longing in those words, but what did they think of the more overt sexuality these women had? How, in fact, would I ever learn what they really thought about modern women, being one myself?

As if to include me more within their group, Margarita began, "I learned this from my mother," and as the pig's guts slopped in the bowl, she reminisced like women do during the holidays, hanging around the kitchen. "In those days we had music and dancing, big fiestas. Of course everybody had nine, ten children..." At once we were there, picturing the guests, the excitement, when people lived in remote *fincas* and there was little else during the dark months but work.

Tia María appeared with a tray of *buñuelos*. Her long face, as solemn and bloodless as an El Greco most days, radiated good cheer while she passed round her gifts. The *buñuelo* is their version of a doughnut: flour, eggs, yeast, (and if you're lucky, lemon zest), kneaded and fried in olive oil. Very heavy, and with their gritty coating of sugar, a bit like a soggy golf ball with prickles. At fiestas, de rigueur. I gulped mine dutifully.

Strangely, there was no one younger than me around. In fact, everyone at this fiesta looked middle-aged, or older. I asked Margarita if the sight of the suffering pig was too much for the youngsters, as it would have been for mine. No, she said, they had all gone, even as little children. Of course the death was horrible at first, but they got used to it, *"a poc a poc"*. Then the woman who was helping her, Carmen, spoke up. "Our children don't want to come anymore, only my son. These days they only want to go to the discothèque," she said. "My daughter thinks this is disgusting," said another, and one by one, they began, intoning something one had been hearing of late, a sort of lament. It spoke of trees scraggly and unpruned, fruit rotting on the ground; of fields left untilled, covered in brush. It was the land itself they were lamenting.

"Who will perform the *matanzas* if your children don't do it?" I said. Even as the words left my mouth, I regretted them, that we had arrived at such a sad note. It was a fiesta, after all. For a while there was only the sound of guts sloshing around the bowl.

"After we die?" said Carmen. "I suppose someone will carry on." Her voice was vaguely optimistic, despite what we all knew. How much they must regret the passing of their way of life, more than I possibly could, yet she wouldn't dwell on it. Acceptance of Fate. It was in their carriage, dignified, impassive, giving them that serenity we lacked in our anxious, goal-oriented lives. Whenever we spoke of the future, of plans, ambitions, anything that hadn't happened yet, both the Marías were quick to add, *"Si Dios quiere"*, God willing. Like the muslims before them: *inshallah*.

The men were not around. No surprise there. For nearly everything, eivissencs formed male and female spheres. Marietta directed me toward a large shed, now a garage, where I found *los machos*, chopping meat on long tables. They didn't seem to mind me poking around, watching, although they ignored me for the most part. To break the ice, and perhaps suggest why I, a foreigner and a woman, might be there, I told them about my father.

Some were salting the fat. These morsels would take time, like wine. "Under a year they don't taste so good," one of them said, and the rest laughed. It was the man I secretly called "Woodchuck" who spoke. Small and stooped, with a very jolly face under the beret he always wore, he looked remarkably like one, sawing logs all day in a shed at the edge of town. He had never spoken to me before, nor had any of them really, except Miguel.

There was a lot of grinding going on at the other table. They were making two kinds of sausage. From their description, I realized that what they called *butifarra* must be the black stuff you saw hanging in *tiendas*, made from the blood and all the organs that contained it. The other, *sobrassada*, brought back a memory, of a couple, Antonio and Eulalia, and their *finca* near San Carlos. We were at their wooden table, each with a slab of bread smeared with bright orangy-red stuff, and I was sinking my teeth into something surprisingly delicious once you got past the lumpy texture. Tangy, and very different from any sausage I had ever eaten.

The men were warming to me now, giving me the recipe: lots of paprika as coloring and preservative, and a bit of black pepper; possibly some ground clove or anise. For *butifarra* one used nutmeg. Remarkably, garlic was not traditional in their *sobrassada*, but skin, ground up into tiny pieces, was. (Ahh... The chewy bits.)

The best cuts were on their way to the fiesta table, they said, or would be eaten soon. Thinking as a modern person, of the gigantic freezers Americans had, it seemed a waste. But from their point of view, it made perfect sense. In the dead of winter, everyone gained in rotation, first one household, then another. A happier idea, really, fiestas, holidays. Back to the Greeks, offering the entrails at the altars of their gods and distributing the meat to the people afterwards.

In fact, the *matanza* was really an ancient and most efficient method of recycling: leftovers transformed into flesh, butchered in winter when crops are scarce and human bodies need meat to keep warm. This pig's sacrifice would feed several people for weeks.

Alas, poor piggy had not volunteered. Despite the logic behind it, and the intoxicating energy of people working together, the spectacle of his suffering remained. "Who killed the pig?" I said. They all chuckled. No one wanted to step forward. Finally a tall man, the one who ran our local gas station, confessed. I watched his hands cutting away at the meat: puffy-looking like my father's, like the pig's.

I risked one more question, the one I had wanted to ask all day. Why didn't he hit the pig on the head first so that the animal didn't move so much (I was careful not to say "suffer") in dying? He was sympathetic, surprisingly so. I guess I was expecting him to tell me to get back in the kitchen where I belonged. "Yes, I know they do it. A shot in the head maybe, or even a hammer. It would be better. I don't know. This is how we do it here - my father, and my grandfather, and his grandfather..."

His words trailed off across the street. I followed them, past the facade of La Isla Bonita to the terraces. A herd of sheep were jumping over the stone walls, walls that had carved out fields of wheat and olives centuries ago. Was there some atavistic wisdom in the way they killed the pig?

I was thinking of my father. We were out in the back garden - I must have been about seven - and our tabby had just appeared with a bird in her mouth. I was running after her, trying to rescue it, crying in frustration. Dad was digging, or pruning bushes or something, and he stopped to look at me. When he spoke, his voice had that gentle tone he used on those rare occasions when it was just the two of us, chewing the fat.

"Let it go," he said. "I know. It doesn't seem fair. Nature is like that, cruel sometimes. We don't understand it, but that's the way it is." I respected my father, and I felt good that he was speaking to me of serious matters, but I was sure I would never be able to just accept things like that.

12

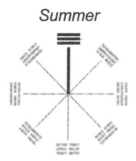

Summer

Shooting Eivissencs

DESPITE THE DEBACLE of my Geldof "scoop" that first summer, I carried on writing and taking photographs. Even though I could see the shot and had the knack of being in the right place at the right time, I knew I was too ham-fisted to make it as a paparazza. I tried offering the island's newspaper, *Diario de Ibiza*, some black and whites of San Pedro matrons, perched on tall ladders painting the church. Perhaps an image from the *campo* might contrast nicely with the traffic accidents and urban news? Whitewashing was a seasonal task, and judging by the age of the houses, it had been going on for centuries. It fell to the women, who got out the ladders in spring, covered their heads, and doused their dwellings with straw brushes on long poles, treating the ceiling beams to a coat of diesel and turpentine as well. The *Diario* editor tossed the prints back across the desk. "What's this? When you've got a picture of Felipe González kissing Princess Di, come and see me."

Then, when we had been there about two years, a photographer from New York arrived, looking for a writer. Barry (let's call him) was putting together a guidebook to the Balearic Islands and through the expat grapevine, he found me. I wasn't sure about the project, at first. Promoting the island to tourists was all wrong to my way of thinking, exactly what I did not want to do. As it turned out, he was aiming for a hardcover edition with fine photography and an educated text; a book for the armchair traveler, and, I began to think, a possibility to get beyond the "Babes and Babylon" Ibiza image. At that time the island was getting to be known as the place where Europeans went for "sex, drugs and rock n'roll". That was the only thing most people knew about it.

As I traveled around the Balearic Islands that summer, what struck me was how different each island is, right down to the bone. Menorca, lying north, is virtually flat. Terrific gales from the Gulf of Lion in France hit this island first, bending trees and bushes right over the rock walls. How dry and brittle it looked after the lushness of Ibiza, boring, until I stumbled upon a *naveta*.

A few centuries after Stonehenge, some mysterious people were building megalithic monuments on Menorca. Theirs were different - T-shaped *"taulas"* like sacrificial slabs and huge *"navetas"* resembling upturned boats. Menorca is virtually littered with them in various configurations, as if a tribe of baby giants had left their blocks behind.

As for the largest island, I ventured forth on a scooter, then realized it would never make it. Majorca's northwest coastal road led round a bend into a cluster of peaks seen just below eye level, like facets on a crystal, then onto a rocky jaw of sharks' teeth before the lighthouse of Formentor. The center was a vast and a lonely-looking plain with huge plantations of cash crops. In contrast to Ibiza with its small farms, Majorca had a feudal look. Farmers lived in villages rather than on the land, and drove out to their fields.

Of course the biggest island had been the obvious choice when the medieval lords of Aragon ousted the Moors and built a kingdom in the archipelago. And for a couple centuries after the Conquest, the capital city, Palma, was a maritime giant running three hundred ships. Then it went downhill economically until quite recently. Thanks to tourism, the Balearic Islands have become the wealthiest of Spain's autonomous communities. The Palma I saw had the self-important air one would expect of a capital city, inside a necklace of beach umbrellas.

Returning from that, Ibiza felt more rustic than ever to me, a country of "hempen home-spuns", never mind all the resorts sprouting on the coast. I had just unearthed this gem, the Creation of Man, as told by the eivissencs:

> When God began to create the first man and the first woman, he brought with him a big angel to help him work the clay and another little one who wanted to help. They all set to work, and when they finished making the man and woman out of clay, they decided to weigh them. Observing that the man weighed more than the woman, the angel made two balls with the clay that remained, and placed them on the woman's breast to equalize the weight. Weighing them a second time, they discovered the woman now weighed more than the man.

Therefore the little angel intervened, saying, "I'll fix this right away." He took some clay from what was left, made two little balls, and taking one in each hand, went toward the man and Plop! But as he was so short, they landed between the legs, and thus were created the first man and the first woman.

[From *Cuentos, Creencias y Tradiciones de Ibiza* by Michel Ferrer Clapés, Ibiza, 1981.]

It was those hempen homespuns we were hoping to capture as we set off to photograph the eivissencs. Barry worked a lot in Asia and often stopped off in Ibiza on his way. He had never lived on the island and didn't speak Spanish or know any eivissencs, so he needed me to find locations and negotiate the shooting. Mornings we would head out after coffee in some quiet bar, usually too late for more than an hour or so of shooting before the sun reached the wrong angle. As we plowed through potholes in his rented wreck, he guzzled huge bottles of beer against the heat. How could he work in that state, I wondered? The trick was, getting ready to shoot, he appeared to suck body and soul into the camera and focus himself along with the lens. Admirable.

Subjects like baking in wood-fired ovens had to be arranged in advance. Sometimes we drove out to spots I knew and looked for likely shots - a woman feeding chickens in the cactus, say. I would get out and after a few preliminary remarks, explain that I was writing a book on Ibiza and would she mind if we took her photograph for it? She would get a picture in return, when we received the copies.

Hardly anyone objected, even when Barry, in bursts of enthusiasm, trampled their crops transporting his gear onto the "set". Old ladies climbed terraces, fed and re-fed chickens while the cameraman took frame after frame of the same picture. I didn't like the method. My favorite photograph at the time, from the Spanish national newspaper, *El País*, showed Daniel Ortega clutching his phone, waiting to connect on his first direct-line to

Moscow. It had that "captured", accidental look. Barry required predictable results: good color, precise focus, attractive composition, with a sort of staged spontaneity, ideally.

Toward the end, we needed something for a vignette on olive pressing. No one knew exactly how ancient this ritual was, but the method and equipment they were using looked as old as Odysseus. It was a communal operation. Only a few farmers had presses, so neighbors brought their harvest in turns and helped. The job involved getting a horse to turn a stone mill that crushed the olives. The mash went into baskets and they pressed them under a massive tree trunk, driving the oil into a ceramic vessel shaped like a figure eight. A dose of boiling water drove the oil to the top and chased the residue out below. The vessel was dubbed the "inferno", and you could sort of see the association, separating things out, the impure, as ever, descending, like those quaking souls above church doors.

Years before, I had watched one of my landlords at the task. Although he was no longer young, Antonio was tall, dark-haired, virile. For him, coaxing his mare around the heavy stone was an act of great *machismo*. Photographs of Antonio promised to be intense and tremendously authentic, more so than some of the others. Barry liked the concept, and we drove off to set it up with Antonio.

His finca lay at the floor of a wide valley, beside a deep *torrente* that flooded with the autumn rains. It was not a large or handsome house; bare stones, rather than stucco, a few pots of flowers on a little concrete patio in front. Chickens ran right up near the door. The olive press stood in a large room alongside the house built for the purpose, called a *trull*. Siesta was nearly over and Antonio was hitching up his trousers on the patio when we arrived.

He was a bit incredulous. Why a shot of that, when we could have his wife, Eulalia, with her flowers? In the end, he agreed, as if it were a good joke. We would have to talk to his *vecino*, of course. The neighbor would be coming with his harvest in a few days.

We found the neighbor a little ways back down the road, a small man, rather nice-looking and shy. He didn't mind the idea, *"si Antonio dice"* - "if that's what Antonio says".

On the day of the shoot, we could hear Antonio shouting to his horse as we drove up. I went in the shed to say hello while Barry got the equipment. The mare looked exhausted already and Antonio was sweating to keep her going. The neighbor looked more fresh, in fact, a little too fresh. Instead of the dirty farm clothes he was wearing the day we met, he had on an immaculate vest, a new straw hat of the *"tipico"* variety, and a brand-new pair of *esparto* grass sandals, the ones they wore now only for dance performances.

What to do? He had obviously bought these things to make tradition more "authentic". "Holy shit," said Barry, under his breath. "I guess we can't tell him to take that off." "No way," I said. "You'll just have to shoot around him."

Barry set up his camera and started working. Antonio was perfect, so involved with the job, he had forgotten about the pictures. The *vecino* carried on with his part of the operation, out of fire often enough, thank heaven. After a while, Barry moved the tripod. He peered through the lens and was about to begin shooting when he popped up, shouting, "No! No! That's all wrong. Cover that thing up!"

"That thing", I discovered, was on the wall just behind Antonio. A brand new geyser for a demand water heater. I had never seen it before. Apparently, for the first time in their lives, Antonio and his wife Eulalia had water running into their house - hot water. I wondered which room they were using for the bathroom (their *finca* had only three) and what it looked like.

Antonio stopped. I told him we needed to do something about the water heater. *"Si, si. No problema,"* he said, *"un momento,"* and he disappeared around the corner.

A few minutes later he returned, carrying a brocade shawl. It must have been part of Eulalia's traditional dress, probably hidden away in a cupboard for fiestas. Old ladies still wore them, their hair in a kerchief with a pigtail out the back, though I had never seen Eulalia in anything other than her everyday outfit. Antonio walked over to the bright white metal object and lovingly, draped the shawl around the sides, like a picture frame. Beaming, triumphant, he stepped back to admire it, and turning to the assembled company, he said, *"Ya está perfecto!"* "Now it's just right!"

13

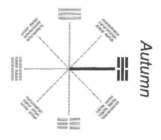

Autumn

Adiós

THINGS WERE NOT going well. In fact there had been no "all clear" on the domestic front for some time. More and more in the wee hours, little people tucked up in bed, our conversations kept drifting toward one thing: staying, or going back. On the bright side, the travel guide was nearly a *fait accompli,* researched and written in just over four months despite the chaos at home. A few days before the deadline, Birdie had bumped into a makeshift desk I set up on the terrace and my vintage Remington went crashing to the floor. An Englishman we didn't even know heard about it and produced another one.

Duke was still our major source of income, and bogged down in a kind of absurdity. After creating a Moroccan-style pavilion and some furniture, he was now brutalizing doors and windows. A wealthy client required "authentic" woodwork for his *finca,* which was being restored. Old doors would be drafty and less secure while new ones looked, well, new. We would beat impeccable surfaces with chains and whatever else was around, then attack the grain with chemicals and wire brushes. Very dispiriting for Duke. As he put it, he was a builder of wooden houses on a island of stone ones. Besides, the money barely paid our bills.

Watching San Pedro in the evening, old boys playing cards in the bar, children running in and out, I would compare that to America as I thought of it: possessions, mostly, and walls, isolating one person from another, swallowing up the elderly in "homes", and I would say that life here, despite the difficulties, was healthier.

It would also be painful to go back. In the small community where we had lived there was work for waitresses and builder's assistants but not much for art historians. Ibiza, provincial, yes, but a place where a great variety of people gathered had generated writing work for me. Going back meant exile, to the kitchen sink, the building site, the woods. Difficult as it was minding children and writing for a deadline, I was thriving as never before.

To be honest, I was attached to Ibiza at the gut, not the head. Photographing with Barry one day, an old woman rattling almonds from a tree dropped her stick, climbed over a fence and came up and kissed me on both cheeks, like a sister. Such moments, when they came, drew the cord tighter.

Then there was that mysterious, almost primeval quality. Midsummer, for instance. However the solstice was celebrated originally, the Christians had turned it into a mass for Saint John the Baptist, a major fiesta. Menorca's celebration, for instance, was a medieval-looking affair with riders in costume and jousting in the harbour. On Ibiza, a row of fires was set alight in the village named after the saint, and one by one, men jumped over the flames. In the dark, I had seen two young silhouettes I recognized, José and Vicente, and many youths I didn't, following the men, running the gauntlet. It looked like something one read about in Frazer's *Golden Bough*.

I would be finishing up the book with Ibiza's neighboring island, Formentera, only twelve miles long and nearly flat. The girls were holding up remarkably well despite being ignored much of the time. For once I had a relatively simple assignment so Vedra joined me. We set up a little tent in some pine trees near the Playa Migjorn, a long stretch of very white sand on the southern coast, and made wobbly excursions on a rented *mobylette*.

Then one morning in October, rushing to get ready for school, Vedra cut her wrist sawing at a loaf bread. I ran out for help. Whoever was on the *paseo* brought us to a door in a new apartment block up the street. The cut was gushing blood and the "doctor" didn't use any anesthetic to put in the stitches. While Vedra screamed - quite natural in the circumstances - he told her to stop making a fuss, as if having one's arm sewn up like a handkerchief were nothing at all.

That, for me, was the turning point, a "sign" that brought everything into focus. Whatever harmony we had found or created was dissolving. The children came first.

By November our family was in departure mode. We would get rid of everything with a garage sale and take the bus from Barcelona to Paris, then travel on to a friend's in London before flying to the U.S. Selling tools would help pay for the trip. Except for one; Duke had lugged his radial arm saw from the states like an alter ego, cramming its huge crate into taxis, trains and boats, and to part with it was, I think, like giving up his profession.

The sale was not as great a success as the one we held in America before leaving. The person who wanted the tools said he would have to return another day with the money. We decided Duke and Vedra would go ahead to Barcelona to ship the saw, and I would finish up our business and join them a few days later with Birdie. Meantime, she and I could stay with a friend.

The day I went back for the deal with the tools, there was something eerie about the snaking cords, the saws and drills heaped on the elegant tiles with their arabesques. Empty of all that had made it ours, the apartment felt alien. The buyer never arrived.

Toward evening, I climbed the road above the village with my camera, remembering vaguely a finca some distance away with a beautiful trellis of bougainvillea. The owner was outside gathering kindling when I got there. At first she wanted to put on her traditional outfit, but posed in the doorway for me anyway: big straw hat, hands on hips, proud, sturdy. Her husband was lying on a sort of palette bed in the *entrada*.

We started talking, as one often did for openers, about the harvest. They would be eating a lot of potatoes for dinner that winter, he joked. I told a few stories about the country rats of San Mateo. "They only eat what they need to," he said. "They don't go out of their way to harm anyone". How fair the logic, I thought, if only one could keep that in mind, staring down a snout at beady eyes.

On the way out, he handed me an enormous bag of potatoes and onions. I felt embarrassed, said it was too much, I was on foot, and so on. In fact, town was about two miles back down the road, but really, it was absurd to take so much of their food. He insisted. I was being shy, and surely, a bagful of food was worth walking a few miles with a heavy load.

Back at the Isla Bonita, the tide was turning. A friend offered to buy the tools and take our cat as well, and there were drinks all round. I went over to the apartment to pack the last things. The moment came. I returned to the bar one more time, shook

Manolo's hand and kissed Carmela goodbye. Then, a bit drunk, I hopped into the car and, trying to to start it, saw our cat crying on the steps and remembered the most important thing: I had forgotten to tell the Marías goodbye.

I ran in. We embraced and cried a bit, and assured one another I would return soon and send news. Outside, it was raining now. As usual, the car refused to start. I climbed out and began to push it out of the *paseo* onto the street. Tia María, who had been watching at the door, rushed to help, and hopping into my jalopy and bidding her the last farewell, I escaped San Pedro. A mile or so down the road, peering through the windshield wipers, I recalled something. As Marietta and I were pushing the car, the bell at the church began to toll. Manolo. Had to be. So there was a soft spot in that unfathomable heart.

Part III: These Days

14

Summer

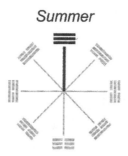

From the Balcony

AT FIRST GLANCE, a balcony is nothing special. Some sport fancy ironwork. Others sprout small forests in pots, but on the whole, if we consider them, isn't it as design elements on a facade, like the shape and spread of eyebrows on a face? That's what I used to think, standing with a friend on her balcony in Santa Eulalia.

These days, the city stretches uphill to the old fortress church and wears an esplanade below a skirt of seaside hotels. When I first saw it, Santa Eulalia was just a string of houses along the road to Eivissa. As the first nightclubs like Amnesia and Pacha grew with techno and rave in the '90s, clubbers began to fly in for annual rites of self-annihilation. Now the Ibiza scene is world famous, where glitterati go for the never-ending party, is the spin. Santa Eulalia lies outside the main venues, but for some years I have been watching its transformation, arriving like a swallow for the summer season.

To get the feel of a place you have to fall in with its rhythms - that's my method, anyway. And so, finding yourself in Santa Eulalia of a morning, you dive among the sweating bodies in the fresh food market, the babbling and jostling, the hooking of a fish and landing it. Then, weaving plastic bags out into the noonday sun, around legs and café chairs, past cars, between trucks, you climb two or three, or even four flights of stairs.

A quick tussle with the key and quite possibly a dog, who is skilled at sneaking out, and you escape into the cool tranquility of an apartment. Soon you are in a tiny kitchen chop-chopping garlic and whatever looked appealing in the stalls that morning.

Just past the stove in my friend's apartment, a door leads out to a rear balcony overlooking a sort of No Man's Land enclosed by the backsides of buildings around the block. The space is festooned with clothes dripping onto fallen toys and rags that wait, like souls in purgatory, for some indefinite rescue. Most days around lunchtime, a child at the east end will be tooting away on his recorder. Then there is a lot of bucket-sloshing, and from various directions, little voices giggling. Trapped within the space, our sounds rise and mingle, as if it were one vast kitchen; as if, mopping, stirring, chopping out the daily drudgery, we in our corners are not alone but adding notes to a communal song, *Mediodía*, midday.

How different the front balconies of the neighborhood, where plumbago and bamboo hide the sunbathers and news readers, who (it is well within the rules), peek at what is going on below. Public it may seem, suspended above the world like a flag, but the balcony in Santa Eulalia is private territory, part of the home, so that while you may look down, we on the street do not look up, *officially*. At the end of a blistering day, one might be wandering around Canon Square, for example, and notice the man smoking overhead is still in his undershorts, having just rolled out of bed.

A Spaniard would never appear on the street this way in a country where every man, rich or poor, "is at heart a grandee", or was in the 1950s when the travel writer, H.V. Morton, described them. Customs change, and of late on the esplanade you will see old boys in bermuda shorts, but the *paseo*, or promenade, that Spanish custom whereby one struts a persona along a public space is as vital as eating on Ibiza.

While those on the *balcón* do not participate in the theatre of the street, as the audience is not on the stage, they are, nevertheless, part of what is going on. My friend is blessed with a balcony that stretches across the entire width of her apartment. There are seasonal rearrangements. Arriving in June you might find its two permanent residents in their turtle tank atop a pile of furniture while the Maestra tests her props. One summer it was the seraglio effect, with the couch at one end enclosed by screens. For about a week, people-watching had a slightly naughty appeal. Then it grew hot and the oppressive blinds went up and down and withered on their cords until one morning, like a dead bouquet, they vanished.

The street where she lives is barely wide enough for cars to pass. Two thick-walled houses survive from the days when men called Jaime and Toniet emptied their nets on what was then a pebbly beach and hauled the catch to a tree not far from the town hall. One of the houses is a restaurant now. In the other, an old woman carries on behind high walls as, presumably, she always has, as if the hotels, the esplanade and all the cruisers in the port did not exist.

Mornings begin with a public announcement from whichever of her hens is trying to lay an egg. Then silence. Days rise slowly near the port, where many have been up half the night. Until the metal doors slide up in the shops around ten or eleven, the street is a vacuum punctured now and then by flipping flops or canaries, blasts from boats to Formentera or sometimes that distinctive ring of butane bottles, dragged across the pavement. Heat hangs without and within like a sleeping pill that hasn't worn off.

How many, I wonder, heard the drunk on the first floor banging for his girlfriend to let him in? Did they also wake with the whooshing street cleaner? The bottles crashing as the bars cleaned up at dawn? Open your balcony to the breeze and the uproar, or close the doors and suffocate in peace: that is the question. Nevertheless, the eivissenques on our street are up with the sun, hanging out their laundry. Sometimes you hear the woman with the chickens hosing the pavement, swooshing away last night's orgy with her broom.

Eventually a car door slams and the day gets underway. By eleven it is in full swing, motors, dogs, high heels clattering along to the shops. One year, sleek machines appeared on some corners, like bellhops issuing tickets. Apparently, the City looked out from the town hall and noticed that the number of cars had tripled. Down below, drivers inch around each other, eyeing short-term spots before the morning melts like ice cream, doors close, and the street empties.

I used to think of siesta as that irritating moment when the shop shuts just as you arrive. Now I savor it: a languor so complete that on our balcony you can hear a pinwheel whirring in a potted plant. A baby cries out between spoonfuls and a distant dog is barking, but it is otherwise so still you can hear two men talking a block away in the port.

According to their elegant ways - dining around eleven, promenading before nightcaps in a bar - sleep is something Spaniards catch in doses. What an asset to digestion, the leisurely lunch, the drowsy lie-down with the paper, fan blowing air from the balcony to the mattress. Has anyone researched the benefits to literacy or health? Plus, you have to wonder, how many little Spaniards are conceived in this swoon of heat and leisure?

Siesta punctuates a day, gives it form: morning jam, slow drift; second rise, final peak, dissolution. Years ago when I lived in a boat on the Thames, twice a day the great surge of the tide lifted us off the shingle. For a vague time we bobbled at high water in a wide and tranquil river beside a flotilla of jetsam. Ducks paddled through, picking things over like shoppers at a car boot sale. Then back out it all went, easing us down until the keel touched bottom, and everything went rigid again.

These rhythms are addictive and I'm guessing that the people around me are imprinted in a similar way by the rhythms of a Spanish day. What impact will it have on family life (so valued in this country) if shops stay open and the workers don't go home for lunch? In *El País* I read about Madrid's twenty-five to forty set, struggling to keep up with the old late-night style while they now spend siesta at their desks.

On Ibiza in the summer season, with more than a million bodies alighting on an island twenty miles long, siesta is the one time-out. Businesses, streets reach critical mass as people hung-over from the night before charge out in the midday sun to refuel before the doors shut. By the time they reopen, foul tempers of the morning have dissolved in the sea or the shower, and, sea breeze rising, bonhomie returns.

Sometimes when a heat wave hits, a kind of madness overtakes me and I must get to the center. After Santa Eulalia, with its clean esplanade and beach full of children, Eivissa at noon is a shock to the system. Debris oozes from the narrow alleys in the port along with the scent of antiquated plumbing. Giant ferries churn diesel into the air. As the shops begin to close, there is some urgency to get out of the sun.

The closest thing to a breezy balcony is the cliffs of Dalt Vila, but today it is too hot to climb. I have wandered into a newer square, the Plaza de Parque. It looks vaguely like old Barcelona, a shady cafe-lined square with palms and mimosas in the corners and a row of orange trees in the center. A good reminder, when one is feeling cynical about "progress", that a few years ago, this was a bottleneck with petrol fumes.

The cafés have only a few customers and like me, they seem to be in no hurry. Nor is the staff. We sit, backs to the wall, gazing across the square where a few bodies stretch out on the pavement with an air of having slept there last night. One is strumming a guitar. Cicadas rise in chorus. Spoons tinkle on saucers around the square.

A kind of camaraderie unites us, slumped, dozing, suspended by a truce with the heat. Chatter fades. Now and then, someone will scuffle through in babouches as if the square were one vast bedroom. A waitress arrives at a table nearby, hair hanging wet from the shower. We extend our legs, sweating, basking in the the scent of cologne on a passerby.

Around 5 o'clock, a sea breeze stirs the blood. We linger, reluctant to take up the getting and spending, I expect. An engine whirrs on the next street. People appear in fresh clothes, sit down at the tables. As if a curtain were rising, we who sat through the interlude turn to each other and begin talking, or pay up and head out, on our own trajectories once more.

The evening promenade in Eivissa builds over several hours, a real poodle parade of tanned flesh in the port. For such a show, a balcony is ideal, the dress circle. A couple hundred years ago, though, this staging was reversed. Because they were part of the home, balconies were one place "proper" ladies could appear in public without an escort. Leaving their peek-a-boo screens "to establish themselves..in the air above the street" was a victory for Spanish women, according to Gerald Brenan.

In 1919, Brenan left Bloomsbury for a small mountain village in Andalusia. A young man at the time, he was interested in mating customs. As he would describe later in *South from Granada*, if they wanted a more intimate encounter with a suitor than the view from the balcony, young ladies had to stand behind metal grills on the ground level. Nowadays when everyone has the freedom of the street, there is little reason to look up, and in the port of Eivissa where the scantily-clad and glamorous stroll by all evening, who would?

The *paseo* in Santa Eulalia, by contrast, is full of families dripping ice cream on their holiday clothes. Tame, but as the night progresses, nearly as loud. From the bar at the bottom of our street come the British favourites "Oh Danny Boy", "I Did it My Way", "La Isla Bonita". Later, it might be wandering drunks. Around dawn the synthesizer from a club in the port is still throbbing. Officially, music is supposed to stop at a certain hour. This venue closes the doors and continues inside until around daybreak.

When the heat and the bacchanal hit the zenith, I wonder what the eivissencs think about the noise. Apparently, going without a night's sleep is a price they are willing to pay, as much for the general bonhomie as for the money it brings in, I think. Of the three-day orgy that rages just below their *balcón* at Midsummer, Marietta sighs and María smiles and throws up her hands. Perhaps they have come to think about it this way: how lucky to attend the fiesta lying down. Of course, when they were young, the sounds drifting over the railings would have been guitars or, more likely, the scrabbling and whispering of *novios* crawling up with flowers for the ladies. Drama, romance, the balcony has lost this terrain to the street. And yet, one stifling afternoon in Barcelona, lost in the dark maze of the Raval, I stumbled into a plaza so far off the Ramblas it had neither tourists nor shops nor any of the Barceloneses one sees in the main parts of the city.

It was a large cobbled square with balconies on all sides and must have been rather grand once. Now it looked forlorn, shedding a layer of posters and paint. Siesta was ebbing. Puffs of air were drawing people out from bedrooms above. A woman in a dressing gown leaned against a railing, combing out her long wet hair, and I began to notice a couple others, half-dressed, gazing down at the only life below: cats creeping along the shaded walls, and me.

As my eyes adjusted to the light, I detected two more people about to enter the square from an alley. Men. Rough-and-tumble, by the look of them. And from a radio somewhere up above the voice, burning, agonized, inconsolable, of a Flamenco *cantaor*. Then it came: this square was territory, a place I had no leave to enter, and wherever I had travelled in my own life, I was an intruder here.

But what to do? Scoot along the side with the cats? Turn back? Like an insect on a large blank wall, I stepped into the middle affecting, I hoped, a gait between nonchalance (she's not looking for trouble) and control (she knows where she's going). As the eyes up above stared, I imagined stopping and with a flick of the skirt, declaiming to the gallery: "I am not just this stranger you see here below. I too have suffered, have lived. And if somehow it were possible, I would rather stay and hear your stories than dine with all the pampered ladies of Gràcia." Etc., etc.

But of course I kept on walking, straight across to the other side and made straight for the buoyant air of the Ramblas, where all pass freely up and down.

15

Summer

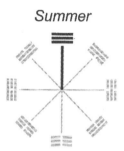

Eulalia

THREE HOURS BEFORE I have to hail a taxi and fly, I spot her. She is at the opposite end of the narrow passage that runs alongside her shop, tottering toward me. The noonday heat has driven everyone, even the dogs, inside. Above us the sun hangs like a flare. There is no place to hide. We shall have or speak, or acknowledge that we don't.

How many times had I escaped Eulalia Noguera? My friend's apartment is just a few streets from her door. Every morning she is on a chair outside her *tienda*, Comestibles C'an Eulerie, sitting while the women sort through her crates, carry onions and eggplants inside to her son. Sitting as crowds storm the pavement, rush to the bank and cafés; sitting as cars pass on the main street of Santa Eulalia, and I, on the other side of the street also pass by.

Once I saw her inching down the sidewalk with her husband. He is a stick in a beret beside her solid flesh, but a lively one. I stood behind him while he bought cake and gossiped in the delicatessen, Can Mayans; she, waiting in front, pressing on her cane. When I went out, they were just up ahead. I ducked behind them and into another shop, as I shoot up the alley when she isn't there.

Each time I see her, I think, "Today I must break through this nonsense," knowing I won't. Yet it is wrong - Eulalia alone, ignored, just another old woman in a chair. Who except me and a few neighbors recognize her for who she is, or was, once. An unheroic age, this, wrapped up in the getting and spending. How many now could sing "*The Internationale?*" But surely Eulalia remembers it, and I wonder if it comes to her, skipping off a Yank's accordion...

It was July of 1936. An American journalist had just disembarked with his family at the port of Eivissa, headed for the town of Santa Eulalia. The American heard rumors passing through Paris but had ignored them. While the Republic might be in danger, Ibiza was a backwater, far away and out of touch. Elliot Paul knew it well. His favorite town was a place "where telegrams arrived in the bus driver's cap." Surely he could squeeze in a visit even if the situation began to deteriorate.

Had he looked at history, Paul might have guessed the future. Midway between Africa, Spain and southern France, in times of war the Balearic Islands could be useful, strategically; had been, ever since the Romans took them from Carthage. Six days after he arrived, the eivissenc commanding the fortress atop the port declared martial law and the fascists took control.

As a foreigner Paul was neutral, officially. Unofficially, his heart lay with Republican friends in Santa Eulalia. For the next two months he cheered them on, helping as much as he could. When they recaptured the town in August, he typed identity papers for their provisional government. His were the first set. Right, left, or neutral, nearly everyone in Santa Eulalia knew Elliot Paul. A few years before, he had been teaching English there, to the town's young women, mostly. Better still, he was fluent in that universal idiom, music. Jamming in bars, he had grown close to the men, teamed up with an eivissenc named Pep Torres. Their orchestra played at fiestas and dances with Paul on accordion and keyboards, Pep on violin and trumpet.

The first time Paul saw Eulalia Noguera she was plucking chickens and singing with the old boys in the kitchen of Cosmi's hotel, very near the spot where her *tienda* stands today. She was sixteen and spirited, more so than the other young women around her. One day she eloped with a chauffeur from Eivissa. The next morning, she returned, alone. Eulalia's family kept her home for months. Eventually, they let her take housekeeping jobs. When Paul reappeared with his family in 1936, Eulalia worked for them.

However people were lining up politically on the mainland, in his memoir of that summer, *The Life and Death of A Spanish Town*, Paul calculates that among three thousand people in the district of Santa Eulalia, there were only a handful, on either side, of genuine communists or fascists. "The rest," he says, "wanted peace". The community as he saw it was neither competitive nor particularly judgmental. Whether one was a workaholic or drunk was a matter of "style." Between farming and fishing, and catering for tourists, no one starved. Santa Eulalia even embraced a free spirit, "the Admiral", who survived happily on fish and wild mushrooms, trading kindling for cigarettes.

Paul's friends - Cosmi, who ran a hotel, three of the four tienda owners, and nearly all the fishermen - were communists, meaning they were for land reform, supported the poor against the powerful, but without following any official Marxist line. Thanks to their sideline - smuggling tobacco from Africa - the fishermen had never been on good terms with the police, who backed the opposition. On the right stood the clergy and the rich, men like Abel Matutes who controlled transportation and cash on the island.

Live and let live was more the motto in Santa Eulalia, however. A few weeks into the war when the Republicans regained control, they brought their prisoners out of jail to attend a fiesta on the *paseo*. Two thousand people sang the *"Internationale"* that day, according to Paul, who was playing with Pep Torres in the background.

As for the women, politics was, by tradition, male territory and they stayed out of it. Eulalia's mother was one exception. The Nogueras were staunch Republicans. Her uncle Edmundo was notorious, so outspoken (especially after a few drinks) the police ignored him, as if too hot to handle.

When the rebellion started, Eulalia jumped in and served as a messenger, running information between Paul and the network. News was hard to get. Radios had been confiscated by the fascists, who controlled the telephone lines as well. Her only source was word of mouth or pamphlets dropped from planes. She may have been the one who organized a petticoat telegraph among women in the campo. A flash of pink, for instance, meant "Danger, search parties about." A brave young recruit, this heroine of Paul's, deploying the only weapons available to an eivissenca as best she could.

One day a truckload of fascists stopped en route to San Carlos where her friends were hiding. Paul describes the encounter. Eulalia "approached the standing truck and looked at the soldiers from left to right, sadly shaking her head and saying softly, 'Well, I had known there were cowards and *ladrones* [thieves] in Ibiza, but not such a contemptible cartload as this.'" She laughed so much the recruits began to fidget, "like hens in a crate." For the American, caught up in the Spanish Civil War, Eulalia was Ibiza's Joan of Arc.

More likely, if she had a heroine in mind it was her feisty patron saint. In the days when Rome ruled Iberia a twelve-year-old girl, Eulalia, was dragged before a magistrate in Mérida. The charge: insulting the Emperor. The magistrate was sympathetic. Deceased emperors, and at that point, even living ones were treated like divinities; as Christians were required to denounce all gods but their own, they were almost obliged to volunteer for martyrdom. He tried to calm the girl. Eulalia, writes the historian Prudentius, spat in the magistrate's eye, "scattered all the idols round, and flung the censers on the ground…"

Centuries later, this Eulalia was also fighting in vain. In August, the Italians stormed Mallorca and headed for Ibiza. Facing the inevitable, Paul and his family escaped on a German ship, disguising his friend Cosmi as their "Algerian cook". Cosmi joined a steamer running food to Valencia from Odessa, while Paul returned to America and vented his grief in a memoir. Eulalia Noguera and her family were left to face the conquerors. *"Es derets van gana* (the Right will win)", she told Paul before he left. But Eulalia was an optimist. "There will be another time," she said.

The survivors scraped by, eating what remained, including the carob beans they had grown for their pigs. The island's modest but reliable tourist trade dried up. A couple decades later, outsiders began to reappear, a small but not insignificant part of the landscape. Whether they recognized him or not, the citizens of Santa Eulalia, for instance, were watching Lawrence Olivier enter an Irishman's bar called "Sandy's".

In the '70s when I first arrived, traversing the island had not changed much since Paul's day. There were paved roads between the three main cities, but the rest of the island was linked by dirt tracks with potholes. Going to Eivissa from the north side where I lived was a major trek. Santa Eulalia might be a weekly shopping trip, if that. I never met the Nogueras.

Seven years later, I returned. This time I had brought my family and, like Paul, headed for Santa Eulalia. That was 1985. Cranes and skeletons of new hotels lined the port, cutting off the old town from the water. The town had reacted with a ban on structures over four stories, but it was too late. Package holidays were bringing them a hundred thousand tourists a year. Where fishermen once hauled in the town's food, a luxury harbor was in the works. Investors local and foreign argued that if Santa Eulalia was reinventing itself, it should "look to Monte Carlo rather than Benidorm". The process that would transform Malaga, Benidorm, and large parts of the Spanish coast was well underway, however.

As it happened, I was writing an article on the effects of tourism and had decided to focus on Santa Eulalia. I had read Paul's book and located his heroine, so one morning I strolled up to Eulalia Noguera and asked her how she liked the new Ibiza. I wasn't sure how I felt myself. It was nice to have a bathroom and to find something other than dried garbanzos in the store, but that tranquility and harmony of the fig-shaded terrace was giving way to the car and the phone booth. New hands and machines were shaping the land by different rules. Perhaps Ibiza had been too generous, was being swallowed by its guests. I think I was expecting a list of complaints, rather like the one my brain was writing up. Of course they must be better off, but the Noguera family, at least as Paul had described them, were not at all money-grubbing.

Eulalia was sitting beside the *tienda,* unadorned as her wooden chair, dark hair swept back, cut bluntly at the neck. The oval face Paul admired lit up at my question. She gestured toward the cars passing in front of us. "We used to sleep with the windows open. Now we can't sleep even with the windows shut." I told her that if she were a grandmother in Miami beach she might be talking lawsuits, or drugs or orgies. She chuckled, as if that were nothing to the eivissencs. *"Pues, bien,"* she said, "if we hadn't had tourism we would all be dead by now. All the young people had to leave to find work."

The old tolerance, laissez faire, alive still, I thought. These foreigners, parading down the pavement in what looked like underwear as if it were their street, were just a spectacle, nothing to do with them. I asked her about Paul's book. "Ah..Señor Paul ... *un hombre muy muy bueno..."* and for some time we sat there, invoking the old Ibizas, hers, and mine. It was the only time we spoke at length. Our family moved to San Pedro, and I spent little time in Santa Eulalia, although we would greet each when we met. Then, a couple more years passed, and we left.

Returning for a visit in the early 'nineties, I found a close friend living in an apartment three streets away from Eulalia's tienda. There was a new *"supermercado"* nearby, plus more hulks of half-completed apartments. Winter loomed in the empty streets, the dead souvenir shops which had multiplied like weeds, too numerous for the trade. It had been a bad summer, people said; worse, everything was more expensive these days. Many old friends had flown, probably for good. We caroused anyway, surrounded by ghosts.

One afternoon strolling toward the *paseo*, I spied Eulalia. She was on her chair beside the *tienda*, as usual, and as I approached, she stared at me, her face completely blank. I hesitated. Something (was it guilt?) hit me. Maybe she had had enough. The commodification of "paradise" - it was happening around the globe, the outcome of rapid travel and free market economics. Whatever our individual intentions, we *estranjeros* had been part of the change. The eivissencs might have contained the process somewhat, but ironically, their "live and let live" style made that difficult, opened them up to exploitation. Perhaps to Eulalia now, I was just another foreigner, a *periodista*, journalist, turning their sad tale to shekels. Like Paul, I loved these people in some visceral way, wanted to belong, but could come and go as it suited me. I was not wrapped up in their fate.

"Buenos días", we said, politely, like strangers. Then, afraid of what she might say, I waved to a friend sitting outside a bar up ahead, excused myself, and charged on. From that day, I began to avoid her, melting into the traffic or walking on the other side of

the street. The pattern was set. I had been repeating it robotically ever since.

Now, years later, here we were, our paths about to cross. I had been steering clear of her for two months, despite renting a car and locating people I hadn't seen since the 'seventies. We reached the middle of the alley. *"Buenos días, Señora Noguera,"* I said at last. Her face - a hollow-eyed mask in the glare - awoke, and she stared into mine. *"Buenos días",* she responded, brightly. So far so good. I asked her how she was. *"Bien, bien ..."* she said, rather like the English say, "musn't grumble". Then, leaning forward, she pressed her fingers into my arm, and added, sotto voce, one conspirator to another, "You know, *señora*, I don't see very well anymore."

Reeling, through awareness, through sadness and regret, I struggled for something to say to her, some consoling words. "I guess there is still the lovely sound of the canaries," I ventured. *"Sí, sí..."* she answered, vaguely. Then, turning to the stranger once again, smiling, "Ah, but *señora,* I still have my husband, my grandchildren, *mi familia ..."*

Familia! Now she had me. To be so grounded, to belong, to know exactly who you are. These days, I told her, my family were spread across the United States. Growing up, my sisters and I walked a few blocks to my grandmother's house where she gave us coffee and read our fortunes from the grounds left in the cup. In my own mind, however, I had always been the alien, roamed the furthest, become a wanderer. My children hardly knew their grandmother. Lately, in bad moments, I found myself pondering the future, having lived in so many places, rooted in none...

We stood there for some time, not so much eivissenca or American now, as two women chewing on life. Then, turning toward her house, and with the natural respect that is the mark of her people, Eulalia Noguera thanked me for visiting with her, and wished me well.

16

Summer

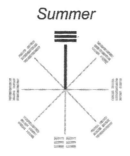

Fiesta in San Pedro

IT IS A Sunday in August and I have been invited to lunch with the landladies. As usual at midday, the smaller door to the landladies' house, the one that opens into the stairwell, is slightly ajar. I rap on it gently. And once more. As I suspect, it is Curly-haired María who emerges from the dark.

Ducking my head, climbing over the bottom step to enter, I can barely see after the blinding light on the *paseo*, but hear her pulling chairs from the table by the door. According to custom, we sit down to chat. She is trembling slightly with the strain of preparing food and greeting me, and after some polite exchanges, I feel I know her well enough these days to suggest we leave the deep nave of the *entrada* and go on in to the informal air of the kitchen.

Francisca, her mother, springs in the back door, followed by Tia María. At ninety, it is the *abuela* who is lightest in body and spirit, her gaunt, slightly stooped frame still vigorous. A few years ago when I learned that Miguel had died and both the Marías broke down, relating the events, Francisca appeared from her room and began to inquire about my children. Time to get on with life, she seemed to be saying.

She thrusts a chair in my direction. The chairs are the old wood and rope ones, very small, and we sit, chests against the tablecloth, María, Marietta, Francisca and me. First there is *insalata russe*, potato salad with brightly colored vegetables and dates. The *abuela* pushes her plate toward the serving platter and shoves a bit toward her. She puts the serving fork back in, turns the plate, and invites me to do the same. We each take a portion in turn.

Some of us chew loudly.

I haven't dined with them for some time and want to talk, but they encourage me to eat while the food is on the table. In any case, we are soon gabbling. First, Francisca. "You know today is the feast of San Jaime, the patron of Spain. But it's not a fiesta anymore. They have taken away the fiestas. San Jaime, San Pedro...people have to work, they say. There was a *missa, nada más.* There used to be a big fiesta. The people brought their mules and horses to the church. The priest would bless them. They put flowers around their necks, and something like castanets - can you imagine the sound? - and they led them around the church three times."

She knows how to bait me. I am always pestering them with questions about the past, but the subject only intrigues the *abuela,* for the most part. I ask her if they went clockwise or counterclockwise around the church.

Rolph Blakstad, who compiled a record of the island over many years, told me that farmers moved counter-clockwise around the threshing floor, as the arabs do at Mecca, and dates the custom to when the Moors ruled the island. The movement, said to preserve *baraka*, or spiritual presence, may have survived in other practices as well.

"They went like this," she says, waving her hand counterclockwise in the air a few times, then when I try to follow precisely, clockwise, peering at me like a schoolgirl who wonders if she's got it right.

When was that, I ask. The three women exchange some words in eivissenc. Finally Marietta leans toward me, her castellano a high-pitched staccato, as always: "No one has a horse or a mule anymore. No one plants wheat. We don't do anything other than collect the almonds and fruits that we can. Before, everything was covered with wheat and sheep and fruit. Everyone says that before long, there will be nothing but pines. *Es una lástima,* (a shame)." Her eyes, more doleful than ever since Miguel died, look away.

I am also sad, I say, to see trees withering, unpruned, fruit rotting on the ground. I know a *pagès* who leaves his farm to work in a bar so he can pay for social security. It is Jaime I am referring to. He refuses to sell the *huerto*, but since Eulalia died, he is the only one left to work it, and can't cover all the things that require cash now.

The old Lament. We've been intoning it for a couple decades. And yet, aren't their lives easier now? When Miguel was alive, María and Marietta were up and off to the *finca* with him at dawn. Passing their door after an evening in the bar, you would spy through the crack a tiny light in the entrada, and if you ever had occasion to go in, the Marías would still be there, hovering around the table lamp hemming handkerchiefs to sell.

These days they manage, cultivating a small garden in back and renting Francisca's *finca*, along with the apartments. Marietta misses the old life, the planting and harvesting with her brother. María's heart is too weak for that now she is often saying, with some relief, it seems to me. Her daughter, Nieves - never a farmer - manages their rentals and has a job in Eivissa. She lives by herself at the *finca* that belonged to Miguel's family.

I look at the aunt. If you could change, get back Ibiza as it was, I say, and the price was to give up the washing machine, the electricity, and the stove, would you do it? "And scrub clothes with my hands again?" she says. I describe how my knees ached from bending over the bathtub upstairs, wrestling the mud out of jeans. We laugh, but sadly, like we do about children growing up and leaving home. Life is easier, but what a loss.

To change the mood, I ask Francisca how she met her husband. Were marriages arranged in her day? I have been reading an account of courtship by an Argentine writer, visiting the island around 1908. He describes a remarkably democratic ritual: suitors queueing to visit an eligible girl; she, wrapped like a doll in fiesta clothes, receiving them one by one, with her father keeping track of the time. Ibiza's historian, Isidor Macabich, also alive in those days, puts the Argentine straight on certain points: the *machos,* he says, worked it out among themselves without the father or his watch.

"Some did what their parents said, but others did what they wanted", says Francisca. She chuckles. Clearly she belonged to the second group. I coax her a bit. "How did it happen then?" "Well, we all had to go to church. Looking here, looking there..." She demonstrates, peeking out from her kerchief, coquettishly. Who could resist her, even now? She is wearing her *traje*, long-skirted traditional costume: shirt, sleeveless overdress and apron - all black, and when I notice it, she says with some pride that she made it herself.

There is a patina that obscures a subtle pattern on the cloth - years of wear, and perhaps today's labor. It's just an everyday dress, of course; she has a finer version for fiestas and funerals. She notices my shoes. "Where did you get those?" she says, like a teenager, ogling her friend's new togs. I am wearing *alpargatas*, suede sandals with rubber tire soles and black strings that lace round the ankle, one eivissenc version of espadrilles. They used to be quite popular with foreigners as well. Someday, when archaeologists from Mars dig up the last two decades, they will note a shift to flip-flops in the mid-'80s. What they will make of that, I wonder?

I stick to *alpargatas*, tough, but whimsical, like ballet shoes. Francisca hops up and tries them on (how remarkably young her feet look!) and I promise to find her a pair in the one shop that still sells them.

After lunch María takes me around the garden behind the house. There are eight *gallos* in the hen house and two roosters in back but the stall where the girls used to bring scraps for the pig is empty. She shows me the trees Miguel planted, lemons and oranges, a loquat and a pear, now bearing fruit. They don't even need to cultivate the trees on their land in the country. "What a terrible thing, Miguel always said. Nieves would never want the *finca*." Now she is living there alone. Since they installed a telephone, fax, computer, Nieves is *"muy contenta"*, could not be happier. If only Miguel had lived to see it, she says.

I wonder. Nieves, the daughter, was the first woman in her family to finish school. Like their contemporaries, her mother, aunt, and grandmother were pulled out of school before, or around adolescence, to work the *finca*. Educating girls was said to be a waste of time, women would be homebound all their lives anyway. This is what María and Marietta tell me. Clearly, it also served to protect their virginity. Swathed in skirts, kerchief, and strands of gold like chest armor, the young eivissenca in fiesta clothes was a face peeking out from an impenetrable mountain of cloth. The next generation - Nieves, in their case - went on to live in Barcelona and finish university. She now works in Eivissa, goes to theatre and art clubs, paints, and judging by remarks she made when we saw her, is part of Eivissa's intellectual scene. Yet tied through her family to the life of peasants. Complete in neither, perhaps. Will she be happy?

Something about Nieves is familiar. It is a Sunday in the summer of 1966 and I am in front of the church our family attended every week, cringing under enquiries from my parents' childhood friends. What was it like in France? Why did I stay there so long? And so forth.

How to explain? Although *Life* magazine arrived every week with photos from around the globe, my family, like the other families we knew, focused on their own community. For me, the pull of "the world" (meaning any place beyond the American Midwest) was overwhelming, and the further I flew, the more difficult to return, heal the breach. How much greater the disparity between Nieves' life and her family's! She never joins us for lunch, even on feast days.

We went inside. I didn't know quite what to do. It was now the hour of siesta and the other women had disappeared, yet for some reason I felt awkward about leaving, as if it were too soon. I suggested she must want to take her siesta.

María looked at the couches in the entrada and suggested I lie down. Had anyone ever done that, I wondered? Until recently, the room was always lined with chairs like a country *finca*. In fact, I had never noticed the couches before. I said thank you, feeling somehow, blessed. As if I were almost "family".

We settled down in the cave-like stillness of her *entrada*, me on one couch, she on the other. I asked permission to remove my shoes. She did the same. It seemed we were making it up as we went along. I lay back, and as my eyes grew accustomed to the darkness I looked around the room, trying to fix it indelibly in my mind. Over the doors of the bedrooms hung the family portraits. There was the grandfather who had gone off to make his fortune in France (a migratory gene!) and the eivissenca he had met there and brought back as his wife. There was also the very odd row of powder blue sabina beams overhead. Nothing to do with Nieves, María said. They had been blue for as long as she or Marietta could remember.

A vast furniture cabinet, eight feet long, or so, displayed the same old tchotchkes: blue and white china, a picture of the virgin, decanters, plastic flowers. These women, rich in property, lived simple lives. The twentieth century had passed through their world leaving a small TV, a phone, and the couches.

Ah, but there on the walls was the daughter's touch, a row of canvases: a still life, a landscape with the *finca*; a woman in white dress and straw hat on a windswept beach, all in an early twentieth century manner, simplified, bold. Modern going "native" interpreted by a native going Modern.

I closed my eyes. We lay together, hostess and guest, while voices and spoons tinkled across from La Isla Bonita, the trucks thundered past, someone sprinted to the apartment upstairs, and the clock ticked away the gap between her time and mine.

17

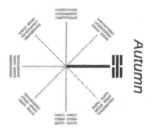

Autumn

The House and the Tree

ONE OCTOBER, FRIENDS *suggested I take care of their house for ten days. What an offer! They lived in an isolated valley in a picturesque cluster of white cubes and tiny windows, an Ibizan farmhouse. Each* "finca", *as they are called, is unique and often quirky, with a pirate tower alongside it, for example, or a staircase where you wouldn't expect one, like under a chimney hood. This one crawled up the side of a hill with eight rooms on different levels.*

Fincas were not built with plumbing or heating or cooking (as we know it) in mind. The style appears to have ancient origins, and the core of a house may be centuries old, with rooms added over time. Authentic ones are hard to come by these days, a pity, because they give the island its distinctive charm. Conversions tend to go for either the "Roman villa" or the "ultra modern" look. My friends' house was beautifully preserved with only minimal adjustments: new floors at ground level to keep out the damp, a solar-powered generator, and a bathroom. It stood above the last bend in the road. A gift from the gods, I was thinking, driving in. As things happen, it was a place I knew well...

Wednesday

Do houses have memories, I wonder, or some imprint of the lives they have touched? Walking around it, climbing on the roof as I did twenty years ago, I feel like a returning ghost. In those days it stood abandoned, and I made secret visits, pictured our family eating in the courtyard under some bamboo trellis we would construct. Then everything changed. Returning one last time before we left, I spied a stack of cement blocks among the rotting leaves. Then saw, like a story told in pictures, the remodeling and the renting. But not to us.

Now a trellis someone else built wears a trumpet vine at one end, like a hat. Many autumns later, chance has brought me back. My stay will be shorter than the lizards', hiding in the garden walls. Yesterday, as we watched a butterfly skirt an ancient olive tree, a friend said: "A day in the life of a butterfly is as a thousand years in the life of an olive." Easy to say, I thought, if you're the olive. But I'll try it.

Summer lingers in the softness of the air. On the patio, a lizard tumbles from the trellis into my lap. Another ventures across the threshold and I follow. We are entering a space as silent as a cave. Or does he hear, in the dark crevasses of the junipers overhead, a city full of spiders?

People sometimes cut huge holes in these houses to catch the view. They're missing it: rooms opening higgledy-piggledy off the main space, light entering through cube-like niches, poetic light, the glow Vermeer caught on the belly of a jug. Walls sag like clay, with no sharp lines or edges. Thick, hand-shaped, then reshaped as each generation lathers on the whitewash. A dwelling cool in summer, impenetrable to winter winds. The badger's den.

Okay, after a wet month, and lacking Mr. Badger's fur, you feel the damp. To stir the blood, you have to get outside. It's cold, leaving the hearth on a winter's day but just out the door is the scent of rosemary after rain, creatures twittering, brightness, life. That old pain/pleasure game - there's something in it.

Never mind winter! Ten autumnal days stretch out ahead like treasure… Back inside, then, to light the kitchen lamp, chop a *calabaza* squash, and put it in the pot.

Friday
Hands around a teacup, I am watching the sun rise above the valley and wondering how much longer this landscape, which has changed so little in the time I have known it, will remain. As the couple who live here revealed the secrets of the house - where the water pump, where the cat food - I asked if they had a radio. They dug around in cupboards and produced a rather useless transistor. Odd, I thought; surely musical people? Now I get it. In this White Noise Age, silence is the most precious music. Already I am wrapped in it like a cloak. Stirring the porridge, I feel the big clock tick, tock, ticking at my back.

Years ago, when I first arrived on Ibiza, sun, moon, and the weather set the pace. Now nearly everyone wears a watch, dashes to work or shop in a car. With time, the shapes farming carved in the landscape are changing. Much of the northern end of the island is protected for the present and landowning eivissencs are wealthier now, at least on paper. Many can afford to hang onto their farms if they wish. Without cultivation, though, pines descend from the hills and swallow up terraces where almonds blossomed. In the infinity of the universe, or even a few generations, will it matter? My mind tries to accept change, my heart, well...

Today, summer marches off with the wind. It's *Xaloc*, the Southeasterly, spinning round the house, tossing the plants in their pots. It bangs the chimes, and flying up, sweeps the sky clean. Birds skitter across the courtyard. Will this wind bring the rains? "Chut-chut-chut-chut," says a meteorologist in the mulberry.

Last night at sunset I took off down the valley and came upon a farmer heading out with a bucket to feed his sheep. I had been looking at his fields, unplowed and stubbly with rocks. It appears he is only grazing a few animals. He tells me he lives some distance away in town, with the *abuela* here alone at the house. Then, rather abruptly, he asks, "Would you like to buy that hill over there?"

It must be very expensive, I tell him.

"No," he says, a bit hesitant.

He doesn't have the air of the prosperous, who rent out houses or run businesses. He's a *pagés*, living partly off his land, filling in with work like Jaime did, with a mother to care for. Difficult.

We gaze at his house. It rises straight from the dirt with no garden. Two graceful arches on the second story, however. Will it have a security gate one day and a vast garage, like a house on a ridge I visited recently? Will the farm become "real estate", something reached by car, fenced off?

I am thinking that when the land is cut up into patches people can no longer cross, we all lose, even if we own part of it. The American solution, parks for hiking and camping, may work in wild terrain but a new "park" on a patch of land near the church of San Lorenzo looks ominous to me. Who needs these picnic tables and signs identifying plants? Ironically, the users may end up to be children from Eivissa's poorer neighborhoods, on rare outings to the country.

Saturday

In the wee hours the night sky is dazzling, Orion bright in the south. It feels ridiculously warm. Pokey, the big tom, circles my ankles as if to ask what I am doing up at this hour. We go inside and lie down to wait for the donkey. Every morning he sends his miserable song across the valley. The Arabs, wrote Gerald Brennan, translate it as, "All women are dead; all women are dead. Oh..here's one." If that is so, this donkey's had no luck yet.

When the rooster crows we get up, Pokey and I, and go out. For the first time in three days the wind drops. Shooting stars drip down the sky. The donkey wails again, even more miserable.

At 7:30 there is enough light to write, no wind at all. My socks soak up the dew. Before long the show begins: pink feathers float across a baby blue sky. A low clump of grey threatens to engulf them, but the rising sun is quicker, transmutes it to rose.

A plane streaks up the stratosphere leaving a long trail. Finally, light hits the trees on the opposite side of the valley. About a month ago that would have set the cicadas whirring but they have been asleep at least three weeks. Dickey bird, who sleeps in a dressing room inside, is very much awake and announcing he is ready for the patio. (Poor canary! He doesn't ever sing.)

Today I'm off to see the landladies in San Pedro. But first, some overripe grapes for the lizards. They are scrambling around in a woodpile by the landlord's shed. Pokey follows close behind, like a child watching the bunny hide Easter eggs. I put some above the rusty scythe, and in two grass baskets for the gecko.

Sunday

A fresh breeze is pushing clouds this way. Last night in San Pedro the air was still, oppressive. Hardly anyone was on the square. All those little people who made it come alive have grown up and left, except for three, and only one has produced an offspring.

I was just saying goodbye to the landladies when Olivia appeared. While we look older, she looks the same, maybe even younger than the woman who used to stand behind the counter selling cheese. She is bursting with her usual enthusiasm and grabs my arm to come and inspect the new flats she's been remodeling. The second story above the old *tienda* is now divided into two: one for her and José, the other to rent. She flings open the door of her one-bedroom rental with a grand "Voilà!"

On an island in the middle of the room, a family of appliances has taken up residence. The stainless steel dishwasher and fridge must be catering size. She is particularly proud of the plasma TV. I realize that while she is showing me the apartment as one would to a friend, she may be weighing my response as potential renter, imagining, I expect, that finally I am seeing the sort of place I would, as a modern person, require.

Naturally I don't tell her I am having a déjà vu: there is María, fiddling with their antiquated gas cooker, and I am studying her, wondering why they don't buy a new one. They could certainly afford it. Now I realize María prefers the one she has, unobtrusive, straightforward. A tool that is a tool rather than a fancy gadget. Prefers her kitchen as it is to the ones in the magazines, as I do.

In the middle of the night, the wind arrives, tossing up the garden I watered this morning. Pots of peppers and plumbago, rose and bay trees, sage and daisies and hollyhocks. Say our family had stayed on, lived in this house. Would we have made such an Eden with our arguments, rambunctious children, our restless selves?

A sleepless night, but tucked up in walls thud-thick and wavy, with a cat at the foot of the bed, who cares? At dawn, an alcove someone built at one end of the room turns mauve. The place, the landlord says with a sweet smile, where he was born.

Monday
Sitting here a decade ago, you would have heard poles rattling the last carobs and almonds from their perches. Now they lie rotting on the ground. Still, someone planted olives on the terraces in front of the house not so long ago. It looks like a bumper crop, if anyone comes to collect it.

With two digestive biscuits and an apple, I am off to lunch with the landladies. I left the car at a friend's house yesterday and hiked back. It's going to be a long, hot walk.

Tuesday
Today it's Migjorn, the south wind, blowing summer back from Africa. That seems all wrong. Plus, I am desperate for news.

Yesterday in San Pedro I stopped at the bar before going to lunch. The place was empty, not even an old boy at the bar. Manolo looked up from the bills and gave me one of his more benevolent smiles. I ordered a tea, and feeling a bit like "family" in this atmosphere, I ventured a question.

"You know, I've always wondered. How old is La Isla Bonita?"
It was the *abuela* who opened it, in 1939, he says.
(That stone-like old troll at the bottom of Olivia's store, with a bar full of men? Remarkable!) "Right after the war?"
"No, *durante la guerra,*" he says.

How could that be, I say, describing what I had read about Santa Eulalia, the shifts in power, the persecution of Republicans. Elliot Paul's book has finally appeared in castellano. I ask if he has read it.

No he hasn't heard of any book by Paul, but how could an inglés know anything about it? There were very few Republicans. Brought in from the peninsula, he says. "The people of Ibiza are very conservative. They didn't want any of this. And it was terrible! They burned the churches.."

He is angry now, and I remember that while Paul's friends were Republicans, he wrote that most of Santa Eulalia didn't support either side, wanted peace. I imagine in a civil war, people are forced to take sides eventually. Who knows what happened in San Pedro? Stable and prosperous decades after Franco died, Spain is finally broaching the topic. Historians and intellectuals might be able to discuss it, but judging by Manolo, who wasn't even alive at the time, old passions lie just beneath the surface.

Across the street, the *albaniles* had strung a huge net over the landladies' house to work on the roof tiles. Ducking under it, I spied the door to our flat upstairs, open, at last! I ran up, and for the first time since our family left, walked in.

148

How tiny, how dull and ordinary these rooms so enormous in memory. Could this have been where half the village children ate spaghetti on the floor at Vedra's party? Or rather, they pretended to eat it, then one by one, dashed back outside. Over in that corner, furious, I threw a book at the wall, and in that corner was the desk with the Remington (old enough for Lillian Hellman, someone said) where the winds of the Balearic archipelago…

I had been almost afraid to see the apartment, imagined all the old passions rising to the surface. But the place we had lived in was gone. Utterly.

Downstairs Marietta opened the door and pulled out two chairs. I was babbling on about going upstairs when she told me. That morning an ambulance had come and taken Francisca to the hospital. The *abuela* was getting very weak. For days she had been rejecting food. Not ill, exactly, just without *ganas de comer*, hunger. We murmured the obvious - Francisca is ninety-something - but what did that prove? She had never been sick, Marietta said, *"en toda la vida."*

Today, restless, I am climbing uphill, imagining doctors with their hard instruments probing this being (surely they are more sensible here, respect someone letting go, if that is what she is doing?) There has been little rain and the land looks much like it does in late summer except for the wilting plumes of sea squill. On a terrace near the top, a desiccated fig lies like a fallen dinosaur, ribs spread across the ground.

Wednesday
"El pasado es al pasado. Seguimos adelante" they were saying today at lunch. María and Marietta do not understand my preoccupation with history and the past. Is it that, approaching the end of life, they don't want to dwell on what must have been happier times when Miguel was alive? Today, however, we were talking about the war. In all the years I have known them we had never discussed it.

Marietta told a story about her father, that men were coming to town to arrest him and he had to hide. *"No mucho - dos o tres días en el bosque"* (two or three days in the woods) but they burned the church and rounded up *"los buenos"*, hauled them off to the castillo in Eivissa and shot them. I asked her who *los buenos,* the good ones, were. *"Los buenos eran los derechos"* (the Right), she said, jaw set, angry like Manolo.

We ate, all quite tired and furtively watching Francisca, who didn't touch her soup. They had sent her back from the hospital. *"Qué alegría!"* we kept saying, whenever the subject came up. What happiness, indeed. The doctors had run several tests. The diagnosis? Old age. *Nada más.*

Thursday

Moving-out morning, lots of sheet-scrubbing in the tub. Just before lunch the landlord arrived. Miguel limped from the car, sturdy-looking all the same. Lifting his trouser leg, he showed off the ankle, so damaged he can't work the farm any more. Shriveled leg, shriveled trees. How painful it must be for him to see his land.

Dickie bird was out for a sunbath, flitting about his cage. Mute as usual. When Miguel heard I had been singing to him with no luck, he shuffled into the courtyard, and putting his mouth near the bars, whistled very gently, over and over. For the first time, the canary put forth a trill, tentative, but something. How stupid of me, singing human tunes. It was birdsong Dickie craved, tunes Miguel knows, of course.

All is in order now but before I lock the door and leave, there is one last visit to make. About an hour's walk away on a slope where pines eat up abandoned terraces, an ancestral olive stands. Bulky as an old bark, it waves a few wisps aloft, all that's left after - who knows? - a thousand years, they say.

Climbing through the brush into the woods, I am trying to follow the old path. Keep running into dead ends, can't find the channel that skirts the side of the hill, as I remember it. Perhaps it's better not to find it, I am thinking. What if the tree is gone? About to turn back, I spot a clearer track, follow it over roots, round stumps, up onto a terrace almost free of brush. And see, across its smooth surface, the Olive.

A friend had brought me here. It was also an autumn afternoon, and we stood apart, admiring the tree for some time. Then, reverently it seemed, he led me around the enormous bole. We marveled at the whorls and knobs, bumps on the old man's body, and the myriad holes and crevices. Doors for what creatures? How many million births and deaths had it encompassed?

Slowly now, I circumnavigate the Olive like he showed me, and reaching out to touch it, I find myself murmuring a sort of prayer. First, a thank you to the centuries of hands that have nurtured it. Then, even though I know it's not the way things usually go these days, that it's not my land, not my tree, I can't help asking. To the hands that would come to cut it down: let this great survivor be, to crumble, feed the life to come.

18

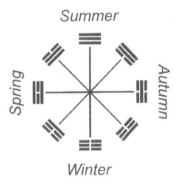

The Source: Returning

WHENEVER I AM on Ibiza, I never leave without a secret ritual. You might call it an obsession and I would have to agree, but there are reasons for it.

The first time I saw the country *casita,* our hideaway in the summer of 1986, it was not the house but the thought of living near Jaime's *huerto* that enticed me. When old Jaime died, there was only his son and Eulalia to farm their many terraces. Cash crops like almonds and carob beans had taken priority over the quick-rotting fruit in their orchard. More and more, the *huerto* was left to spin its own course. As the trees spilled their riches onto wildflower carpets and vines slithered up the unpruned branches, the orchard was evolving into the sort of place you entered through the back of the wardrobe. Titania's bank was how I thought of it in those days, ordinary life and all its thorny hedgehogs, banished. Except for Pep, of course.

The *casita* had no such lyrical qualities, nothing other than walls, a roof and floor. Water gushed by in a cement trough on the other side of the patio, but as that only worked when Jaime opened the irrigation system, every morning the girls and I climbed up a track through the *huerto* to the spring at the top. A couple times a week we hauled our buckets full of laundry and washed it on stones in a little reservoir nearby.

Up there it was utterly peaceful, the girls playing in the water, birds chirping along with the frogs; such a relief from those dreary mornings in town scrubbing clothes in the bath. Sometimes I would look out across the valley daydreaming about centuries of women and children following the same path, coming here to wash. Were we in this way keeping the place alive?

Like a mother, the spring fed its children. Outside the chamber a large stone basin served thirsty animals. Below, and dribbling like a mouth fit to burst, a reservoir held the *fuente's* great gift until Jaime opened its spout and water gushed down troughs to the terraces of the *huerto.* Down to the cherries and apricots, on to the oranges and lemons, and last, to the persimmons. Halfway to the bottom, where the trees yielded to grapevines, a lofty palm swept its head full of dates across the sky. From the spring up above it

155

seemed to reign over the valley. There was something tremendously ancient about that tree and the *huerto*, some quality, that set them apart from the surrounding land.

Years before, researching a medieval manuscript in the British Library, I would be scrutinizing urgent, funny-looking little figures, working out who might have painted them, and as my mind wandered, I tried to imagine what it was like, living in the twelfth century. Then more pressing needs intervened, and leaving England in 1976, I thought I had closed the book on all that. But at the end of the journey, there were the eivissencs, ploughing with horses, scything by hand, looking, despite their button-down shirts, suspiciously medieval. What a joke.

But Jaime's *huerto* was older, I suspected, bearing fruit even as his ancestors took Ibiza from the Muslims. According to one story, what enticed the Christian conquerors in 1229 was the succulent food from Majorca they sampled at a dinner party. Of course, the Christians had other reasons for setting sail - pirate raids on their shipping, for instance - but the prize had to be worth fighting for. Like modern allies looking for oil, they made a pre-conquest survey of farming on the biggest Balearic island. The results were impressive.

Hidden under a tangle of brier at Pep's house was an odd oval structure, like a well, except it was about seven times the size. The opening was blocked off by timbers. I never thought much about it until I began to notice similar skeletons around the valley and learned they were something called *norias*, mule-driven wells where water gushed forth in buckets strapped to wheels. *Norias* were just one of the irrigation systems Muslims brought with them when they conquered Spain in the 8th century, technology so productive it fed legions of scholars and artisans in Córdoba and Seville.

One day when we were living by the *huerto*, I came upon Jaime opening the sluice to the reservoir. He explained how it worked: each farmer down the hill got an equal turn; if they needed more water they had to wait until the next time. "Old as the Arabs", he said, standing a little more upright, but was that just a way of speaking?

As I would discover years later, it was indeed an old system from Syria, designed to fulfill one of the first laws established by Mohammed. The "gift of water" requires a Muslim to share it with man and beast. Underlying this law is a belief that communal wellbeing is more important than individual rights. Quite different from our Western notion of property rights where wells are concerned.

Watering crops is a more subtle problem, of course. As Islam spread to farming communities, local customs and differences in Sunni and Shia practice shaped irrigation laws. And yet, even as private rights to certain sources were upheld, the community prevailed. When Muslims took Ibiza in the tenth century, they transformed vast areas of the island into lush *huertos* like Jaime's - orchards planted with vegetables and flowers, farmed by family clans. Jaime's spring was one of those nourishing an entire settlement, a *venda*, they called them.

That must have been a great time to live in Al-Andalus, Muslim Spain. The Arabs in power, the Emirs of Córdoba, ruled with a policy called *convivencia*, religious and ethnic tolerance. Arabs, Christians and Jews were living side by side (if on separate streets). Growers were importing lemons, date palms, apricots, and saffron from the East and creating, in palace landscapes, the Muslim vision of paradise: a shaded and orderly garden, perfumed by fruit trees and flowers. From the center rose the life-sustaining sound of water, flowing down channels like blood from the heart, the gift of Allah to men. Jaime's *huerto* was hardly a palace garden, yet it had the same symmetry and order, with water running between terraces either side, and many of the trees praised by the poets of Al-Andalus: pomegranates, pears, oranges, lemons, cherries, and plums.

As Christians recaptured Spain bit by bit, the layout of the land began to change. On Ibiza, the new rulers wanted taxes in durable crops like wheat, oil, and wine. Women started small gardens beside their houses for family vegetables, as they do today. While the *norias* remained in use, the land was split up into smaller holdings. When Spanish ships returned from the New World, they brought the agave, whose giant spikes punctuate the countryside like creatures from the moon. Today, only the ghosts of Al-Andalus remain, hulks of abandoned *norias*, a few *huertos* like Jaime's, the perfume, as you walk down paths at night, of orange and jasmine.

So, like a friend you begin to understand over time, the *huerto* took shape for me. And yet, long before that little paradise was laid out, the spring that fed it was there. Scooping up the water, I always felt the sound rushing over, through me; not alive, exactly, but present. I never mentioned that to anyone, even Jaime.

Getting to know him and Eulalia happened *poc a poc*, little by little. One afternoon, the girls and I returned from a hike to find them harvesting potatoes near the *casita*. There were only two of them, hard at it, and as we started talking, it seemed the natural and decent thing to pitch in. The sun was riding low, as I remember, but not low enough. Before long I was well-broiled and wishing we had gone to the beach, or visited friends, or anything else that would have kept me from this labor. Meanwhile Vedra and Brigid were having a fine time showing off. They were used to work from the years of building our house and rushed back and forth, gathering up little seed potatoes.

Around sunset we finished. Jaime lit a fire with pine branches and as the twigs turned to coals, he threw some of the potatoes on to roast, along with red peppers. Eulalia went up to their house for olive oil while Jaime showed us how to scrape off the burnt pepper skins and then, at last, we all stretched out on the ground, feasting on their version of potato salad, and the evening breeze, blowing away the sweat of our labor.

After that, there were visits. Formal ones, by invitation, with stiff entrances as we all put on our best manners. Once we sat down and the bread slicing began, everybody relaxed. Jaime was a sensitive man. He must have been around thirty then, tall and long-faced like his father, but sober, like his mother. He believed in self-sufficient farming, praised, as we ate, the island's traditional way of life. Unfortunately, more and more they needed cash to survive. Jaime pruned trees for foreigners who had bought *fincas* nearby. Eulalia never talked about it, but I heard from other people she occasionally did housekeeping.

Farming was giving way to tourism, land disappearing with developments. Jaime and I jabbered on about alternatives without having any idea what might actually work. Saving the landscape depended on farming, not a lucrative job. The *huerto* needed several hands, plus transport and organization to get the fruit to market. Whenever I mentioned getting married and having a family, he laughed. "No eivissenca these days wants to be a peasant."

The following year, in December, we left. I would send them our news from America in letters tucked into Christmas cards. They never replied, not that I expected any. In the early '90s I began to return, every two or three years for a few days, visits too brief for the trek to their *finca*. Finally, around 1998, I walked into a cinder block hole between two empty restaurants and rented a car. As I turned off the highway onto the long dirt road that led to Jaime and Eulalia's, I wondered what lay at the other end.

A country road one has walked many times becomes a poem. Any intrusion can put the rhythm out of kilter, for better or worse. With every bend in the road, each familiar *finca* or olive tree, I began to forget the ugly marks along the bigger roads, or at least, put them in perspective. At the very end, after a twist to the left sends you skidding up a little rise, their *finca* stood, inviolate. Chickens scrambled into the cactus as I pulled up under the lemon tree by the gate.

I presented a new flowerpot from town, remembering how Eulalia treasured the jug I passed on to her when we left, chipped spout and all. Now, a bit embarrassed, I noticed several large, much finer pots around the courtyard. She bustled into the kitchen to make *buñuelos* while Jaime showed me around. They had done some renovations, he said.

At one end of the *entrada* stood old Jaime's winepress, a bit too clean. Obviously it hadn't been used for some time. Otherwise, the *finca* looked rather as I remembered it until I began to realize that the great river of stones across the *entrada* floor had been tidied away with a layer of terra-cotta tiles. "New floors, a new roof, *nada más*," Jaime was saying, as we stepped down into the *cocina*. Lost among a sea of gleaming tiled surfaces, Eulalia was stirring her *buñuelos* at a wooden plank set on trestles, as if camping out in her own kitchen.

Hours later, we were standing on a rock wall above the *huerto* when I looked down toward the spring. An iron door was bolted across the archway, blocking the entrance. Jaime read my face. "We had to do it. You know, people are ignorant. Since they paved that road, the cars keep coming. Crazy people. Garbage." People left soap on the steps, even shampoo bottles in the spring, he said. All the neighbors had keys now. I could take theirs any time I wished...

I had been struggling to swallow it. Walls blocking off land, tarmac slashing up valleys. But in that moment I felt the enormity of the loss. The very soul, it seemed, was slipping away.

I began making ritual visits to the *fuente* whenever I was on the island, as if it were some ancestor's grave and I was the only one tending it. Jaime would be there, but then Eulalia died and Pep went into a nursing home. The brush Pep's goats used to eat began to overgrow the paths. Green sludge floated in the reservoir, choking the openings in and out.

Then one Sunday, sipping coffee at a friend's, I opened a weekend edition of the *Diario de Ibiza* and a color supplement dropped out. It was a segment from a new encyclopaedia of antiquities being compiled by local scholars. As it happened, this one was devoted to wells and springs. There was the old *fuente* at Jaime's, a clump of dead grass around it, along with photographs of several others on Ibiza. The brief captions to the photos mentioned a custom (no one knew how old) of dancing at springs and wells on certain saints' days. Out of fashion for decades, dancing was making a comeback in the spirit, I suspected, that eivissencs had been reinstating their heritage, as folklore that was now "interesting" because it was defunct.

How odd the *fuente* looked in print, flat, ordinary. Nothing like itself. I decided to track down some of the other springs, wondering how they related to Jaime's, what I might experience there. Some were partially hidden by overgrowth and not easy to find. Some were cut abruptly into a slope, dark inside, with moist stone walls and just a couple steps before the water. Often the openings were ogival or parabolic in shape, like half an almond seen edge-on. A few were so narrow that entering was like squeezing back down the birth canal toward a womb-like pool of water. Whoever shaped these, they seemed to have in mind some connection between spring and womb, water as the source of life.

On the outskirts of Santa Gertrudis, I spotted a sign for a well called Pou D'en Gatzara. Having just passed a ghetto of new flats around the main square, I was remembering the ghost town where a taxi dumped me on a sweltering day in the '70s. The driver refused to go any further. Fresh off the boat, a diagram to a house someone had drawn for me, I had slumped down under a tree, no idea where I was or how I would reach the house where I was supposed to stay. Eventually, out of nowhere, an Italian buzzed up like Mercury on a *mobylette*, and offered me a lift.

We must have passed by here, I was thinking, turning onto a dirt road that led to a stand of pines. A fresh-looking sign from the regional government announced that one was standing, more or less, at the geographical center of the island. The well had a simple round housing with a slightly domed roof. It was thickly whitewashed but lacked a bucket; more of an artifact, like Jaime's winepress. I peered into it for a bit, hearing, sensing nothing. Then I looked down toward the base. Despite a grove of trees and an entire field at their disposal, someone had deposited a tidy pile of excrement along with a bit of toilet paper, waving like a flag in the wind.

Perhaps they meant no disrespect. Someone drunk, or a person ignorant of water except as it came out of a tap. And perhaps I was, well, obsessed with this spring and water business. Even so, it struck me as a sacrilege - defecating beside a water source. Or at least, a deep estrangement from nature and life.

Returning to the States, I always stopped for some research at the British Library to prepare for the classes I would be teaching. That summer, I couldn't resist a peek at the subject of ancient springs. What had people thought about them in the past? It was the sort of question that usually leads to a bottomless pit, but as it happened, I didn't have to dig too far. There were several fairly recent studies on sacred sites in the ancient world, including water sources. Not only the Greeks, but Phoenicians and Romans along with the indigenous people of the Iberian peninsula believed that certain springs were oracle sites where one might seek advice from the gods. Others had healing powers. Some fonts combined both functions. Springs dedicated to the Greek god of healing, Asclepius, for instance, used an oracle as part of the process.

On the peninsula, springs were often associated with female divinities. Prehistoric offerings like money and animal remains abound at certain sites. Colonizing Greeks and Romans absorbed the cults, transferring them to their own goddesses. In Galicia, for example, Romans "recognized" the local water deities as versions of the nymphs, who symbolized for them, creative forces. Judging by inscriptions left at some of these sanctuaries, they were especially popular with women.

In fact, springs and wells were some of the most common sites for oracles or healing among ancient Mediterranean people. Sacred sites for goddesses were often in relatively remote locations with springs nearby. At that time, people believed all water originated underground; springs, it seemed, might be direct channels for communicating with forces in the underworld. Whether all springs were treated as sacred sites is another question, but at least one spring on Ibiza was, and perhaps more, in view of who the players were in those days. Phoenicians, Carthaginians, Romans, all had been attracted to this island. The Romans even claimed the soil had a special power to repel snakes.

In a remote cave above the northeast coast, hundreds of images of the Great Mother Goddess of Carthage, Tanit, have been found. The site, called es Culleram, has a spring along with a cistern built at the entrance to the cave, which was used as a sanctuary by the Carthaginians. One offering refers to an oracle associated with the goddess. Did some Carthaginians, or Romans, who took over the island, go to other springs, to Jaime's *fuente* (it would have been just a bubbling pool of water then) seeking an oracle or healing from a divine power?

In his detailed notes on Ibizan folklore, Rolph Blakstad drew what he interpreted as sacred symbols inside some spring chambers. The paintings are nearly obliterated now and without excavating for more evidence, one cannot say. But here's an odd thought: until a few decades before I arrived, belief in a sort of water magic was widespread in Spain. On the night of St. John the Baptist (Midsummer's Eve), the power surfaced, in rivers, the sea, even the dew in Spanish fields. People went out to drink or bathe in it. At some locations, nymphs came out of springs, they said. (When the great Lope de Vega was writing plays, his hero, Manfredo, was overcome by a whole squadron!)

Three hundred years ago, if you happened to be in Andalusia on Midsummer's Eve, drawing well water at midnight, you might have glimpsed a vision of the future. By the 20th century, it was simply a matter of washing your face at sunset to be more beautiful, and then chucking out the basin in the right direction. Isidor Macabich, writing down the island's folklore at the moment it was fading, explains that the first man to tread on the water would be the beloved. If you lived near one of the sources dedicated to St. John the Baptist, you might have been going there at Midsummer to dance. Jaime's *fuente,* I should add, was one of those.

So what do I imagine I encountered at the spring? you may ask. I cannot say. Only that to this day, whenever I descend those steps, raise its water in my hands and hear the sound, an experience of something greater than ourselves haunts me there.

Sources

Ibiza & Formentera's Heritage: A Non-Clubber's Guide by Paul R. Davis, Barbary Press, 2009.

The Road to San Vicente by Leif Borthen et al., Barbary Press, 2007.

The History Buff's Guide to Ibiza by Emily Kaufman, Tarita S.L., 2000, and her article, "Sharecropping in Ibiza" published in *IbizaNOW*, September, 2003.

The Phoenicians and the West by Maria Eugenia Aubet, 2nd edit., Cambridge University Press, 2001.

Iberia in Prehistory by María Cruz Fernández Castro, Blackwell, 1995.

Correspondence of Walter Benjamin, 1910-1940, edit. G. Scholem & T. Adorno, pp. 389-394, University of Chicago Press, 1994.

Cuentos, Creencias y Tradiciones de Ibiza by Michel Ferrer Clapés, Ibiza, 1981.

Historia de Ibiza by Isidoro Macabich, Editorial Daedalus, Palma, 1966-7.

South from Granada: Seven Years in an Andalusian Village, by Gerald Brenan, 1957.

The Life and Death of a Spanish Town by Elliot Paul, Random House, New York, 1937.

Archive of Ibiza, Rolph Blakstad, unpublished.

Oracles, Springs and Religion in Spain and the Ancient Mediterranean

Oracles, Curses and Risk Among the Ancient Greeks by Esther Eidinow, Oxford, 2007.

Native Religion Under Roman Domination: Deities, Springs and Mountains in the North-West of the Iberian Peninsula by Elizabeth A. Richert, Oxford, 2005.

Oracles of the Ancient World: A Complete Guide by Trevor Curnow, London, 2004.

An Archaeology of Natural Places by Richard Bradley, London, 2000.

Religions en la España Antigua by J.M. Blázquez, Madrid, 1991.

The Gods and the Place: The Location and Function of Sanctuaries in the Countryside of Etruria and Magna Graecia (700-400 B.C.) by Ingrid Edlund, Stockholm, 1987.

La Estación de Amor: (fiestas populares de Mayo a San Juan) by Julio Caro Baroja, Madrid, 1983.

Islamic Gardens, Irrigation Systems, Water Rights

Gardens, Landscape, and Vision in the Palaces of Islamic Spain by D. Fairchild Ruggles, Pennsylvania State University Press, 1999.

The Design of Irrigation Systems in Al-Andalus by M. Barceló et al., Universitat Autònoma de Barcelona, 1998.

The Islamic Garden, Dumbarton Oaks Colloquium on the History of Landscape Architecture, Washington, 1976.

W*ater Laws in Moslem Countries* by Dante Augusto Caponera, Rome:
Food and Agriculture Organization of the UN, Land and Water
Development Division, 1973.

Ibiza: Archaeology, Architecture, Springs and Irrigation Systems

Inventari del Patrimoni Hidràulic, by Joan Josep Serra Rodríguez,
Consell Insular d'Eivissa, 2005.

Guía Del Patromonio Arquetectónico De Eivissa y Formentera by Pere
Marí, Susana Cardona and Xescu Prats, *Diario de Ibiza,* Ibiza,
2003.

Acknowledgements

First, I am deeply grateful to the Hon. Brigid Campbell and Penny MacInnes who made this project possible.

Warm thanks are due to Peter Unsworth for permission to use his painting on the cover, and to Peter and Jenny Unsworth, Anna Brooks, Jenny MacCrae, and Linnaea Phillips for their generous hospitality at different stages of the project. For their critical perceptions, I am indebted to Professor John Callahan and to Martin Davies, who was especially helpful during the final stages.

The late Rolph Blakstad shared information and ideas on many occasions and kindly offered the use of his library and notes. For insights regarding S'Hort, I wish to thank Selim, Gita, Joachim, and Rosanna Minopoli. I am also grateful to Marta Matas Espinar, who kindly transcribed the playground rhymes for chapter eight, to Emily Kaufman, for sharing information, and to Charlotte Firmi for help with points of translation. And thanks to Grace Morgan and Geoff Fisher for their work during the design phase.

I wish to thank the people of my village for their kindness, especially María Ferrer, a longtime friend. For encouragement at different stages of this project, I am indebted to many friends, especially Tony Peake, Karen Heaps, Chris Smith and Lisa Rosenbaum, Susie Tomlinson, and Cassandra Meagher. Warm thanks are also due to the late Mary Blakstad, and to Patsy Dodd, for the initial spark.

Especially I want to thank Michael Kauffmann for inspiration and encouragement in turning my scroll into a codex.